BLACK-WOMEN RINGS AROUND SATURN

BLACK-WOMEN RINGS AROUND SATURN

Clyde Yorkshire

ISBN: 9780578826172

BLACK-WOMEN RINGS ON SATURN

"Black-Women Rings on Saturn" is the perfect way to start this story, the tale of a young boy's incredible journey into Pangaea after it became Middle-Earth during the supermoon Titan of Saturn; this moon was the size of Texas and has been the shepherd of Middle-Earth for three ages of mankind, which lasted 6,060 solar years. This magical journey begins in the womb of a black woman—the fight to protect the future ages from mankind and the reptilians. The child was chosen to come back down to Middle-Earth after Pangaea was destroyed below the firmament and above the abyss from the melanated sun as a human being; the queen of the universe placed the rings around Saturn and a six-pointed star, a hexagram, before the shepherding moons were created. The rings around Saturn and the hexagram were a Tartarus-like condition; Pangaea was a place created by the queen of the universe for melanated beings before Saturn turned it into Middle-Earth for mankind and reptilians. On October 28, 1980, in the Western Hemisphere, in a place called the United States of America, the child was set to be born in Mount Sinai Beth Israel hospital in Manhattan, New York. This was the child's second solar return to Middle-Earth, through the portal of the woman's womb; mankind was expecting him, so the queen of the universe changed his arrival time, so the child traveled in the universe heading toward the star gate; the only entry from the universe into Pangaea's flat earth plain is the woman's womb. The queens of the universe sheltered him and moved his birth from 3:41 a.m. to 4:44 a.m. Eastern Standard Time because of the radiation microwaves in the antepartum room. His celestial vessel he traveled on had a vibrational frequency of 7.83; the hospital equipment prevented his arrival; his story begins in the woman's womb. The queen of the universe downloaded the child's previous life and destiny into the embryo; the warning of Saturn was given to the fetus, his eyes open in the womb—the conception of consciousness.

ANTARCTICA, ARCTIC, AMERICA, AFRICA

The game of life in Middle-Earth hemispheres is often interrupted like breaking news, a sudden reminder to the occupants on the face of the earth that the eye of the queen of the universe is beaming down on humans and mankind like the rays of the sun; as we dine in the pale moonlight with the most luxurious fantasies from north, east, west, and south, the constellation of stars remains the same, no matter what compass or navigational device one chooses. I suspect even if a man could live six millennia with a rainbow of inventions, the golden sun and silver moon still would remain a mystery to us. I believe that business, education, and religion act as a buffer, preventing the master of ceremonies from illuminating the simplicity and accuracy of the constellation classroom. The obvious discovery of the very hand of God is science; the active force, or Holy Spirit—the breath of life—is a euphemism for science. I needed answers to satisfy my curiosity about religion and civilization (both claim to originate with God), so I went to a local bookstore in my community. I have never been to a bookstore before; like many things in our neighborhood, foreign nationalities operated all the commercial businesses; black people didn't have any idea what was in our community because we didn't put it there. So all the ethnicities from foreign countries became refugees because of US foreign policy, and interest came right to the black community. The foreigners turned refugees filled their bank accounts off of the poor newly freed black slaves who were a part of the Peter-pays-Paul agenda. The idea was the United States would empty the foreigners from their countries through proxy wars, and before the displaced refugees could realize what had just happened to their war-torn lands, they had become the owners of new homes in the United States and merchants in the black community. The black community being fresh out of slaves, with very little knowledge of domestic and foreign modus operandi, hoped to gain its freedom and respect helping to create refugees out of the foreigners. The black community didn't know anything about the foreigners it was fighting or that this was all a part of a bigger plan of the white community, the business of creating refugees. After four hundred years of slavery and restricted access to global affairs, the black community assumed it was fighting for freedom against evil people across the ocean. With no international relationship or authority as a sovereign nation, the black community had no choice but to help its former colonizers and slave masters. This veil of ignorance over the black community came about through religion and civilization; both operating systems pulled the wool over its eyes. I walked past the bookstore; at first it appeared to be going out of business; the place looked abandoned. The windows were very dirty, with a sign I could barely read that said Closed for Business, but the front door was slightly open.

BOOKSTORE VIRGINIA

I opened the front door, and the bell above the door frame didn't ring; it just knocked against the glass. I called out in the bookstore several times ("Hello? Anybody home?") with no response. I walked inside yelling hello. Still no answer. I was hoping to find a book on prehistoric plants and animals and human beings like Lucy in Ethiopia that predate biblical writings and civilization, the things archaeologist have found embedded in Earth's rock. I figured that would be a great place to start—a book on fossils. I looked around the bookstore aimlessly. I decided to come back another time, so I walked back toward the front door. I noticed some large maps on the wall I'd never seen before in school or the library; written on the maps was "Pangaea." The maps show a different Earth, one with all the continents together like one big landmass; another map showed moonlike spacecraft destroying and separating the land, forming continents on that map; the name "Middle-Earth" was written. One of the maps caught my attention; there was a picture of giant black women wrapping chains around a planet; the name on that map was Saturn. I assumed that was the name of the company that manufactured maps. This antique bookstore had many interesting and fascinating artifacts. I yelled out again hello; the store was empty. I walked toward the cash register; there were dust particles everywhere. I was confused because on the counter there was an invoice dated 1952 and a notepad with the words "the flying saucer conspiracy"; somebody had been here recently. I noticed a blue-and-white coffee cup, the Greek kind, on the counter; when I opened the lid, I felt the heat coming from the cup. I smelled cigarette smoke too. I saw a pack of Lucky Strike smokes on the counter; most people I knew in the year 1999 didn't smoke Lucy Strikes. Most people smoked Newports, Kools, or Marlboros. The store looked like it had been closed for over twenty years; the floor was very old, and the ceiling had many cracks. I could see the back of the store because of the sunlight beaming inside the holes; with dust everywhere, the place itself was an antique. I could tell by the ladder attached to the bookshelves that it was time for me to go. I had spent enough time browsing about; before I could walk away, I noticed a black cat walking in the back of the bookstore, rolling around on the floor, and meowing a small little kitty. I'm sure it was hungry. I called the kitty; as I bent down to call the cat, its eyes were glowing bright green, then blue and orange. I didn't know what to make of the strange cat; obviously this was someone's cat. I noticed a silver collar around the neck of the cat; as it got closer, I noticed a round-shaped object attached to the collar shaped like the planet Saturn; the black women were putting chains around on the map. I assumed the charm was a little bell. I picked up the kitty to see if it was male or female; it jumped out of my arms and walked toward the back of the store. A light coming from a hole in the ceiling in the back of the store shone on a black box in the middle of the floor in the back of the store. I'm pretty sure it hadn't been there before. I walked toward the back of the store to get a closer look at the black box. The black kitty lay next to the square. I got on my knees to examine the black box. I wiped the dust off the top of the box. I noticed engravings in the middle of the box; there was a four-way compass inside of a circle initiated at the tips of the box: "N"; "E"; "W"; "S." The top of the box read "Pangaea," and on the bottom of the black box there were also four squares; each one had an "A" in the middle of it. I picked up the box and carried it to the front of the store. I stopped in my tracks because I noticed an old black woman sitting behind the counter reading a newspaper with a cigarette burning in the ashtray. I couldn't believe my eyes. I hadn't heard anybody come in the door. I walked closer to the counter; in a soft voice, I said, "Hello. Excuse me. I'm sorry—I was looking for a book. The front door was open." The old woman kept rocking in her chair, and the cigarette kept burning. I walked toward the cash register to hand the black box to the old woman and apologize. The woman's hair was white as snow; she had to be at least eighty years old. I didn't want to frighten her. I didn't get a chance to explain what I was doing in her store because of her apparent hearing problem. I left the black box on the counter and walked toward the door.

The old woman said to me, "Are you bringing the books to the back door for delivery?"

I said, "I'm sorry. I don't understand." She asked if I was the new delivery guy. Not to worry her, I played along. I slowly came to the conclusion that the old black woman had Alzheimer's. I noticed the newspaper the woman was reading, dated 1952, looked different. She asked me to lock the back door when I was done with the delivery. I walked to the back of the store to close the back door—that was the least I could do. I locked the back door. I heard music playing in the front of the store. I walked back toward the front of the store. The little old lady was playing German music from the 1920s; she asked me with a sad face if I would dance with her, and she called me Hank and said her family didn't visit her. I felt sorry for the little old lady. I didn't know how to say no—her family or friends were properly too busy. She asked me again as I was thinking. I said OK.

She said, "Thank you, Hank." I figured one dance, what the hell. I asked her name while we danced. She said Virginia; I told her my name was William. We danced for about ten minutes. I asked Virginia if she wanted to feed her cat; out of concern, I was willing to help. She said, "I don't have a cat." I noticed a collar or necklace around her neck identical to the one I had seen around the cat's neck; the ball attached to Virginia's necklace read Saturn. The music stopped playing. Virginia slowly walked back behind the counter. I walked toward the front door. Virginia yelled, "Hank, wait a minute. You forgot something." She handed me the black box. She said, "You're forgetting your work. I said to her that the box wasn't mine. Virginia shoved the box into my chest and said, "Now don't be late for dinner, Hank." I must've been tired. I could've sworn Virginia's eyes turned green like the black cat. After leaving the book store, I walked toward the Brooklyn Navy Yard, where my dad was working. I needed a ride home. The book store was ten blocks away from our apartment. Walking home wasn't easy; every block had a pack of stray dogs that patrolled the neighborhood. Getting home took lots of effort. I made it just in time to Dad's job at the navy yard.

Dad was walking out the side door into the parking lot. He was happy to see me. I was happier to see him; those dogs was a pain in the rear end. On the way home, we stopped at the fueling station. I loved the smell of gasoline; my dad always let me pump the gas as long as I didn't tell Mom. My sweet Christian mother was very superstitious. Splitting a pole or breaking a mirror was a big deal to Mom. The gas station was more dangerous than both of those combined. Mom made us pray before and after we left the gas station. Usually, ten dollars filled the tank. When I got back in the car, Dad asked me where was I coming from.

I said, "The bookstore next to Mr. T's barbershop." Dad asked me what I was doing over there—that place had been closed for over ten years and boarded up. Mr. Hank's bookstore had been the after-school hangout. Dad said that's where he and Mom had met. The place had closed after Ms. Virginia died (Mr. Hank's wife); she had fallen from the ladder while stocking the bookshelves. I told Dad, "That's not possible. I met Ms. Virginia today. She gave me this black box, and I danced with her." Dad slammed on the brakes and pulled the car over.

He was very angry, telling me to stop it, knock it off. "I don't want to hear any more about this again." The car was silent. Dad make a broken U-turn. We drove past the bookstore; just like he said, the place was boarded up. We made it home. I went straight to my room with the black box. I placed the black box under my bed. I lay awake the entire night. I was so confused. I didn't think about being afraid; I drifted apart in a night of deep sleep—my second out-of-body experience. I heard a noise coming from the kitchen. I jumped out of the bed and walked into the kitchen. I felt every step of the cold floor. The faucet was dripping; I shut the spigot off. The clock in the living room was unusually loud. I peeked around the corner dividing the kitchen and living room; it didn't occur to me that a burglar wouldn't waste thirty seconds in our apartment—we didn't have anything. My heartbeat and footsteps were so loud. I went back to my room. I was already lying in the bed in a panic. I tried to get back into my body. I examined my astrological body. I separated from my physical body. Something at the bookstore had gone wrong my—chakras weren't aligned. I looked under my bed to see if the black box was still there.

BLACK BOX MAP

On top of the box, there were four squares with an "A" curved in the middle of each one. The first was Antarctica; the second, the Artic; the third, Africa; the fourth, America. I opened the black box; inside was a map divided into four hemispheres, with three animal pieces—a polar bear, a hyena, and a penguin—and one person, a baby. On the bottom of the polar bear was written "South Pole"; the hyena, "East Pole"; the penguin, "North Pole"; and the person, "West Pole." On the map were a sun and moon with smiling faces attached to a dome-like glass covering the map with stars spread all around the dome like a rainbow in Zodiac constellation shapes. There was a pair of dice marked "proton" and "electron," with no instructions. I reasoned the map had something to do with my condition; on the four hemispheres was written "of one came many." I was willing to roll the dice. I needed a drink of water. I wasn't thirsty, more like worried. I walked into the kitchen, opened the refrigerator, took the jug of water out, and poured a glass. I couldn't taste anything. I dropped the container and cup on my foot. I didn't feel anything. In a panic I walked outside my apartment. I ran down the stairs to the front of the house. Out of fear I tried to grab everyone I came in contact with. I wasn't able to touch flesh, only their clothes. I sat on the bench outside of our house confused and stressed, watching life among the living. A black cat walked up to me, slowly rubbing against my leg. I was able to feel and touch the cat; it was wearing the same necklace of Saturn as the little kitty and Ms. Virginia in the bookstore. Before I knew it, many cats came to surround me and rub the bad energy off of me. I tried picking them up, but I wasn't able to touch them. Some children from the neighborhood were walking by and started throwing rocks at the cats. I begged them to stop; they couldn't hear me and kept throwing rocks until the cats left. The kids throwing the rocks turned red from head to toe; the other children watching stayed normal. This surprised me; it was puzzling. After the children stopped throwing the rocks, there skin went back to normal. I walked away observing the community. While I was standing near a public phone booth, a couple I have seen before in the neighborhood were arguing. The man struck the woman. He immediately turned red; the woman remained normal. I walked in the middle of the street and stood spinning around looking through a 360-degree paradigm; all the people who were turning red were smoking crack and stealing, alcoholics, and drug dealers. All the people who were turning red were intentionally wicked, consciously hurting themselves or others' it appeared the people's iniquities were highlighted. I walked into a local church. The members were normal, but the pulpit of the clergy was red. I walked outside to observe the police. Some were red; others were normal. I became very disturbed when I look toward the sky; the sun and moon were both out at the same time. The sky was both day and night, like a split screen; the sun and moon both had a face and were yelling at each other. I'd never seen that before. The strangest thing came to my mind. I felt alive, and everybody I looked at seemed dead and in pain; sickness, anger, and violence were everywhere. I followed an ambulance to a nearby hospital. Kids were screaming and crying; elderly people were sick and coughing. It was like a graveyard of dead bodies in every other bed, from gunshots and stabbings and drug overdoses. I ran back to the house ten blocks away. I didn't break a sweat; nor was I tired, remarkably. I went back in the house. Watching the sun and moon fight scared me; the stars were cheering on the fight. Some just watched like witnesses. When I sat down to the map, the water on the map was marked "abyss."

BEGINNING OF THE MAP

I grabbed the dice in the middle of the board. There was a four-way compass I tried turning, but it didn't move. On the board were four cards shaped as squares with an "A" in the middle of them. In the middle of each one of the ace-like squares were written the rings of Saturn; each one had a letter in the top of the ring ("N," "E," "W," "S"). Inside the rings were the elements water, fire, land, and air. The four hemispheres stood for the divide of the people of what became Middle-Earth once Pangaea was destroyed by the lord of the rings, Saturn; on the map, there were dozens of moons labeled demons. When I left the house, the clock was at 4:44 a.m.; when I returned to the house, the time was the same. I checked every clock in the house, including the cable box. Talk about confused. I sat down on the floor in front of the map, an image of Saturn surrounded by dozens of moons, all different colors, with a dragon holding a black square box. Saturn had a large eye in the middle of the planet. I threw the dice down on the map, and the compass spent and stopped with the arrow pointing south to Antarctica with the ring around it. Nothing happened. I tried to pick up the polar bear. I wasn't able to—that was weird. The pieces were stuck to the map. I tried each piece; the eagle and hyena were stuck, but the penguin was able to move. I read the words on the bottom of the penguin: "South Pole." One of the squares illuminated, surrounded by water, with an "A" in the middle of the ring glowing. My room instantly became very cold, then freezing; my room became completely black. I ran out of my bedroom and fell into ice and slid into the water. I panicked, trying to swim and scream for help. I had never learned to swim. I went under the water after about thirty seconds. I calmed down because I was able to breathe in the water. The water was beautiful. I was able to move with so much mobility that it was like flying in the water. I felt like I stayed in the water for hours. I wasn't sure where I was; my instincts pushed me to the top of the ice. My unusual abilities were amazing.

PENGUIN

My eyesight was weak at first. I couldn't see anything. Everything was white—I assumed ice. Slowly my vision came into focus. I could hear penguins. I also heard the sound of a lion or tiger, maybe a bear. Once my eyes focused, I saw a sea lion coming toward me; my instinct pushed me to follow the other penguins, to where I wasn't sure. This was frightening and fun. I didn't know why I was running from a sea lion. I had a good feeling I wouldn't find out. I spent hours all over the ocean. There were so many colors. The illusory paradisial atmosphere was a cantrip. Nature is wonderful. I was learning so many things about the circle of life from the ice. The temperature and climate were in harmony simultaneously with the thoughts of the life-forms in Antarctica. What mankind perceives as tragedy are energy clusters. Everything in nature is aware that there's no such thing as death or hate, and malice doesn't exist. Eventually, I discovered that my physical structure was in the form of a penguin; consequently, this exceptional experience kept me in denial. The diameter of time was expedited. The sun seemed to rise faster than usual; years were like months. The only thing I possessed was my mind. I conceived the process of purpose to never covet anything except your mind. There's so much to appreciate about life. We didn't consider ourselves as penguins. That's mankind's opinion. We're an expression of life. Mankind's society is destroying itself because civilization has created a system with multiple parts religion, school, and work; they aren't from the universe. They're systems of artificial intelligence—the consumption of narcissism. I stood out from the other penguins even though I saw myself through the ice. My reflection bothers me. After five years I accepted who and what I'd become. Eating was very difficult, although the food was delicious. My mind was civilized. I realized I had to become uncivilized. I rejected integration. Letting go of civilization isn't easy. I kept thinking I would wake up from what seemed like a nightmare or shape-shifting gone wrong. My grandmother used to tell me about humans that shape-shift. I made every attempt difficult socially and culturally for the colonies to receive me. I was a vegetarian in my previous life, so it was a challenge to become a carnivore only. I got adjusted after some time; my favorite food was krill shrimp; the squid was high-end, good quality, expensive—not every day we got to eat the high-end things. Our daily diet consisted of a wide variety of fish. I liked crabs, but I didn't have enough experience on how to eat them. I was considered a part of the king penguin species. There were about twenty-five major relatives; our antecedents were great before mankind. The greatest of us was the emperor penguin, then the Adélie penguin. There were also chinstraps, the wise guys; the Gentoos were the most beautiful female penguins. The macaroni penguin was the upper class of the societies, the fancy-pants; their sounds were perfect. The south rockhoppers were the warriors; those guys were legends. The story was that the greatest of them had killed a whale. The north rockhoppers knew all the secrets of the ice—the intellectuals and the wisest of us. Then there were the erect-crested. Very spiritual things were very different. Within the animal kingdom, mankind spoke of heaven and hell; we believed in the great Pangaea to restore the architectural alignment of the earth and bring balance. Pangaea was the mother of the earth, also known as Mother Nature. The penguin believed that the enemy on the planet was mankind and that civilization was a weapon used to destroy nature. The natural order of things was in the biological community. They believed that civilization was breaking the interconnected environment of elements; this systemic extinction had destroyed the Pangaea connection, separating the tectonic plate into many pieces; all energy came from the ground out of the sun. The separation disconnected us from our mother's umbilical cord. I had thought animals talking were just cartoons; on the contrary, we thought and communicated using vibrational frequencies—the way life was intended to. This took time to learn. The planet was in tune with each frequency. There was no such thing as animals or insects; they were all workers or employees of Pangaea. I started progressing the more I comprehend and grasped mentally. The language of mankind was poison to the mind and disconnected humans from Pangaea; all life-forms on Middle-Earth spoke of a time when humans spoke the vibrational frequency of Pangaea, during the age of the pyramids and before the enhancement. The human mind was extraordinary; they could communicate on a high vibrational frequency perfectly. Pangaea was made up of technology and science. Every tree and river mountain was connected with technology. Every wind, ocean wave, and sunray was the technologic science of Pangaea. The contraptions and so-called inventions of mankind had destroyed humans and made the Middle-Earth plain. Every grocery store, restaurant, car, refrigerator, radio, and television had no place on Pangaea, so mankind had corrupt humans with books and computers; those contraptions they called education and religion were resistant to the electrical conductance of vibrational frequency forbidden in Pangaea. Movie theaters, skyscrapers, paper money, and businesses were violations, and even clothes—machines removed humans from the umbilical cord of Pangaea, causing intelligent life-forms to become artificial wasteful disasters on Middle-Earth. Plastic and oil were hazardous materials; cell phones and vehicles were direct results of the fall of humanity. Humans weren't made to create, only cultivate and reproduce. The only creator was Pangaea. Everything on Middle-Earth had become toxic to all created. Everything mankind had invented was a disrespect to Pangaea; it was so obvious in the wars on Middle-Earth, the extinction of life. Middle-Earth had created defense systems, weapons of mass destruction guided by the lord of the rings. Pangaea provided natural defense using tornados, hurricanes, floods, volcanic eruptions, rain, hail, and heat waves. Pangaea had been created before Middle-Earth. Every life-form was connected to an energy distribution grid; this system powered all plants, fruit, vegetables, and water. Pangaea converted energy from the sun into the life-form so we could feed off of different expressions of the sun. This implantation was the rebirth of everlasting life—this process of energy. Pangaea wasn't complicated except maybe to compromised minds. I concluded that I was never leaving the Antarctic until I became a part of the purpose realignment of the chakras of Pangaea—out of one came many. I had two friends, Patrick and Paul. I didn't see myself or my brothers and sisters as penguins anymore; we were an expression of Pangaea. The ceremonial custom of a chosen soulmate was required. I chose Priscilla. She was beautiful but patient with me and communicated well. Her family didn't approve. I wasn't considered enlightened to all the vibrational frequencies and laws of the colony. Priscilla and I talked about everything. I even explained to her I that had once been a human, I don't know if she believed me or not; her reply was that we all had our journeys in Middle-Earth to get back to Pangaea. Every life-form in Middle-Earth had celebrations dedicated to Pangaea; for the penguins, during the festival of Pangice, all colonies gathered together for competitions.

FESTIVAL OF PANGICE

This acknowledgment of Pangaea brought many blessings and peace to those of us trapped on Middle-Earth. I didn't want to compete. I didn't feel welcomed by the colony; Patrick and Paul were my only friends. This went on for years. Priscilla's brother Prone was the alpha penguin; everyone aspired to be Prone, and his friends made every day of my experience a nightmare—plus Priscilla's family had high expectations for her. I was an embarrassment to the colony. I didn't come from a respected family; my etiquette was terrible. The colonies considered me to be a rejected orphan. I told everyone my parents had died at the fins of sea lions. That wasn't unusual and understandably explained my lack of customary training. Prone and his bully buddies were preparing for the competitions the next day at the festival of Pangice; they represented our tribe. The night before the festival, each family held local events in preparation for the competition: swimming, ice gliding, and high jumps out of the water. I failed every year to qualify for the festival; even the females did better, I couldn't even watch Patrick and Paul sit with Priscilla's family; they were very popular. I wasn't given a name by the colony, so I didn't feel I belonged. That evening I decided to do some exploring of the ocean; it was forbidden to go deep into the abyss. My curiosity got the best of me. I went deep into the ocean, and deeper, until I felt a sudden fear come over me, mainly because I had come across a well-lit city at the bottom of the ocean. This ancient city was far beyond the boundaries of the surface dwellers. I could be in trouble with the elders. My eyes beheld marvelous sites, rainbow lights, and pyramids; there was even a moon at the bottom of the ocean abyss. The elders had said it was the workshop of the queens of the universe; there were millions of glowing plants and creatures that lit the abyss—some said even humans were there. I just needed a closer look at the city. I had found a city named Israon, the city of light. The city had two suns. Curiously I moved around the city concealing myself; there were so many black human women and no men. Some were mermaids, and some had legs. All of the black women had natural hair with lightning flashing from it; they were going in and out of a laboratory-like facility, which caught my attention by the red flashing lights on the top of the building. The building was made out of some kind of liquid glass. The women kept coming in and out. With no doors, there was only one window I could see, and why had I looked inside? There were men in huge glass tanks. The women were creating them part by piece. I freaked out in a panic because I was one of them. I saw my old human body. Two women spotted me, and I dashed out of there so fast that I lost my sense of direction. The women seized both of my fins and ushered me back toward the surface. I dropped a crystal Priscilla had given me to be her soul mate. The women never said a word and released me at the seashore. With their heads emerged from the sea watching me, I asked in my vibrational frequency, "What are your names?"

They responded, "If you return, you'll never see the Antarctic again." In my vibrational frequency, I asked a second time. They said, "The queen of the universe knows all things."

The third time I shouted, "What is your name?"

They answered this time in my mind: "The southern oracle." I heard a noise coming from behind me. It was Patrick and Paul. They asked who was I talking to. I pointed at the ocean; there was nobody there.

SOUTHERN ORACLE

Patrick told me that everybody was worried about me. The elders all over the colonies had heard about where I had gone—nothing was secret around here. Paul said the precelebration was cut short. I had ruined things again. Vibrational frequencies traveled to all colony species; a committee was assembled of all the colonies. Before I approached the assembly of elders, Priscilla's dad said aloud, "You're a disgrace to this family." I hung my head in shame; the committee questioned me for hours and interrogated me. I never revealed what I had seen. The committee showed no mercy on me. I was to be escorted to an iceberg for one year, with no contact from any families. The elders sentenced me to leave the day after the festival of Pangice. Just like that, I'd became famous for all the wrong reasons, My survival was in my fins. The community excommunicated me; everything was done through the community, like feeding protection. I had screwed up things badly. Early the next morning, the festival began; afterward was the great feast of Pangice. Once a year the family ate together and discussed the future. Prone was winning competitions left and right; he was loved by the community. Prone was liked and admired; there was talk about him becoming a chieftain right under the elders. I wasn't jealous, but I was no fan; halfway through the game, the ice horn blew. Reports came from the seagulls that the sea lions were planning an attack. They informed the elders of the invitation, but the elders felt the seagulls had plans of their own and couldn't be trusted completely; plus the elder had a truce—this was the constitution of Pangaea, made during the ice age. The queens of the universe, also known as the gods, had created a covenant between all life-forms, like a code of conduct, in the prehistoric days. This agreement is called Pandora's box. At a certain time of the year, no flesh can be eaten on land or in the sky or at sea. The festival continued; so did my misery. Tomorrow I would be taken to the glacier prison, known as an iceberg. Most penguins never returned from the iceberg in the glacier. Prone's favorite part of the games was about to start, the ice rocket—launching out of the water as high as possible onto the ice, this showed the strength of the males. The judges were biased toward Prone; he was winning competitions with his eyes closed. The last competition before the great feast had three rounds. The first round was arguably contested, but the round went to Prone. He made a 360-degree spinout of the water. The second round was a repeat.

The crowd cheered, "Prone! Prone! Prone!" This was the last of the games. The girls were preparing for the feast of Pangice. I have to admit I was having fun as the third round got started. All ten contestants went underwater; one by one they shot out of the water like a rocket. The last one was Prone. Everyone was waiting to see what clever stunt Prone would close the competition with. Everybody got on their feet, chanting, "Prone! Prone! Prone!"—even me finally. He came up and went back down—what a show-off—and again he went up slightly, then back down. The crowd stopped chanting. The seagulls flew by shouting they had gotten Prone.

FESTIVAL ICEBERG JAIL

Dozens of sea lions jumped onto the ice. Everyone scattered like a stampede. Prone didn't stand a chance. I had nothing to lose. I charged water at the sea lions like a torpedo. Two sea lions were pulling Prone in different directions like a rag. I glided into the biggest seal with my beak and poked the other seal in the eye. I grabbed Prone by his fins and pulled him onto the seashore. All the commotion brought the dolphins out; they were the policemen of the ocean. Immediately the sea lions vanished. Prone was badly wounded. The sea lions destroyed the fest and took what they could. Prone was rushed to the ice-pital, the equivalent of an emergency room. What had happened was unacceptable by the international community of the seven seas. Word spread all over Middle-Earth. It turned out that the sea-lions were a group of thugs, a gang of pirates. The dolphins rounded up the thugs with the help of the sharks and seagulls. They were brought to justice by their elders in Pangaea. The ocean was regulated by law and order. My sentence was placed on hold because of the situation. The circumstances surrounding the invasion became a priority. Prone was going to make it. He had suffered minor injuries. Prone's main illness was being mentally traumatized. The community decided to reconvene the proceedings of the festival the next week; after all, this was a celebration of thanksgiving to Pangaea. I wasn't off the hook. My heroic, grandiose, bold behavior didn't change the community perception, especially the presentation the prosecutors had made against me, which was seared into the memory of everyone indelibly—unpleasant and irreversible. I helped set up the festival the night before and worked through the night; this was my community service, I presume. Early the next morning, everyone made their way to the festival of Pangice. The climate was a little different. The week before had left a bad taste in everybody's beak. It didn't take long to lift the spirit back in the community. We were a resilient species. Prone was the guest of honor and keynote speaker. Prone deserved the glory; he was a survivor. I could tell Prone had been able to bounce back even stronger; he coped well with difficulties. This had made Prone even more powerful; his popularity was greater than before. The head priest awarded Prone with the metal frost for his bravery and courage to fight off the sea lion and save the community. All the colonies began to chant, "Prone! Prone! Prone!" Most of the females in the colonies wanted to make Prone their soul mate; finally, the high priest called Prone to speak to all the colonies, which cheered from all territories of sovereign families.

Prone took the stage; surprisingly, he started the speech by saying, "This award doesn't belong to me."

The high priest tried to stop Prone by saying, "Surely you don't mean that." The injury must have confused him.

Prone said, "No, the boy saved my life. Nameless boy we've

rejected, come forward." Everyone turned to me—all of the colonies. I walked slowly toward the ice stage. Prone demanded I be given a name and be acknowledged by all colonies. The elders and high priest formed a huddle, just like the great huddles of the colonies during winter storms.

Before Prone could finish speaking, the high priest said, "That's enough, thank you." Prone limped back to his family. I stopped as well and walked toward the back of the colonies. I didn't have a family. The high priest, Poseidon, said to the colonies, "Under our law the boy is a criminal and shall remain nameless." The colonies started booing and throwing snow; then Poseidon said out of fear, "Wait, we also have to pardon his punishment." The colonies started booing even louder; the high priest was up for election. Every three years a vote was taken. Only elders could become a high priest; the priest could remain permanently as long as he won reelection. Prone stood up and started booing. I felt I had caused this problem, so I ran away deep into the glacier. At the wrong time, a storm moved in and became a blizzard. I couldn't see anything, being covered in snow up to my beak. My body was almost completely frozen. The blizzard covered everything. I was dying.

I heard a loud voice in the air saying, "Say my name" twice. The third time was in my mind.

I said, "Southern oracle." My eyes closed, covered in snow. I woke up the next morning in the middle of a huddle surrounded by my colony. I had made it back somehow. The elders finally gave me a name from the colony: Prime. Priscilla family gave us a beautiful wedding, and Prone gave me his blessings. Patrick and Paul were right by my side. The family was planning a reception for Priscilla and me. There was only one problem: I had lost the family crystal from Priscilla. It belonged to her fathers. I felt loved and purpose; almost a year later, Priscilla and I had our baby chick. We took turns sheltering Presley, our baby boy, in our pouch. The family was coming over later to our place to see Presley. Priscilla's father was coming over to bless our home by formally presenting me with the crystal. I had excepted my new life as a Penguin and my family. I didn't want to go back to my old life. Prone was proud of me. Suddenly I had the life he wanted. Early the next morning, I told Paul and Patrick partly what had happened with my crystal. Later that night we met at the seashore. We decided to catch some seahorses to take with us for light. The lower the seahorses go into the abyss, the more they glow; it may be out of fear. Taking Patrick and Paul was a bad idea, but I needed help. They didn't know I had dropped the crystal in the abyss. The underworld has many names: hell, Hades. Sheol is one of the oldest names of the abyss. *Sheol* means "the womb." I'd been to the abyss one time. Black humanlike woman controlled Sheol. The city was beautiful and dangerous with just the women. The sun under the water was so amazing— to see the great pyramid under the ocean. The legend was true: it was bigger than all the pyramids on Middle-Earth put together.

PYRAMIDS MOON SUN UNDERWATER

We made our way to the bottom of the abyss. Patrick and Paul had never been this far. By the looks on their faces, they were surprised to see the abyss had lights. The abyss was very different from the old story of the lake of fire, Gehenna. The story was true; there was a lake of fire, not for burning people but making land and island. The closer we got to the bottom of the abyss, the brighter things got; there was day and night in the underworld of the abyss. I found the crystal right where I had left it. I put it safely in my pouch. There was liquid glass covering all the buildings; the women walked right through them. There were no doors.

Patrick pulled me and said, "Let's go." I just wanted to look through that window of the laboratory. Inside once again were the men in giant glass cases. The women were creating and studying them; the men were attached to umbilical cords. I even saw myself and panicked. The two women from before saw me. I tried to get away, but my spirit was so weak that they tied me down to a bed. I could see my body in the glass tank's eyes even open. The women were running some tests on me. The moment the women left the room, Paul and Patrick grabbed me, but I was so weak. Finally we left out the abyss. By the time the women returned, we had left just in time. There was a loud laugh in the water, like an earthquake of women's voices. The laugh was the most frightening thing I'd ever heard; it was thunderous and seemed to follow us. We made it back to the colony. All three of us promised to never speak of this night again ever. Priscilla was waiting up for me. She didn't know where I'd gone. Priscilla was worried, and my son kept her up. Presley. One day this crystal would go to him. It was very important to receive the crystal.

Priscilla and I stayed up talking, watching the stars; she said to me, "I know you come from up there. I do believe you."

I told Priscilla, "It doesn't matter where I'm from. This is my home now, and I have a beautiful family that I love." We watched the stars together for hours, laughing and reminiscing about when we had first met—how goofy I was. Horus was rising (that's what we called the sun). The horizon stood for our love, which was growing. We went back in the house and lay next to our son, Presley, on both sides. I fall asleep watching my beautiful family.

In between my sleep, I heard the voice of the women, the southern oracle, say, "You can never return to the Antarctic." The voice said over and over, "We told you never to return." I woke up. Finally the voices stopped. Slowly I looked around my bedroom. It took me about two minutes to realize what had just happened. My mind was trying to register and process what I was feeling. I didn't want to believe that my family was gone and I was back. The time was still 4:44. Right outside my window, the sun and moon were side by side, arguing it was both day and night, and both of them had faces. The more I stared at the stars, they looked like people talking, observing Middle-Earth. They were watching us like fish in a tank. The only way I was going to figure out what was going on with me was to complete the journey on this map. I took the black box from under my bed. The penguin had disappeared off the map.

PENGUIN OFF THE MAP

I picked up the hyena on the map. It was the only peace that wasn't stuck to the map. I rolled the dice and read the bottom of the hyena: "East Pole." My room turned black and became very hot. I felt my atmosphere changing. Out of fear I opened my bedroom door and ran out of the room into Dinknesh in

Gambela. The skies were red as far as the eyes could see; the land was on fire from the thunderstorms; the lightning strikes were dangerously close to our den; the inferno was spreading faster also, as fast as the darkening sky. Today Dinknesh is known as Ethiopia. You could smell the rain days before it came; the fires burned the surface landscape down to a scorched dry ground; our den was near the river where all the herds migrated to because of the water. My mother was the matriarch and the head of our clan, and her right paw was Helen the bone crusher.

The queen was the dominant member of our community. The fires frightened me. I was only a little cub, but the heavy clouds, filled with months of rain and lightning, didn't look good. The water fell from the skies like a waterfall; our den was too close to the fires. Now we had a new problem. This overwhelming deluge flooded our den, so we moved farther away from the river. The clan depended on the females to make good decisions. Dinknesh was one of five countries in Africa that the hyenas controlled on Middle-Earth. Usually the lions ruled.

Cush is now known as the horn of Africa in parts of Ethiopia. The queen was very wise in our clans' wisdom, passed down through the females, especially the Matriarch. Every night was story time. The queen would share the secrets of Pangaea before it had been turned into Middle-Earth, before mankind had enslaved humans. Finally, we found a den a half kilometer away from the river. The den had once belonged to the lions. The smell was atrocious. We had lots of work to do. The odor was extremely unpleasant. Our first night in the new den, the queen told us of the three layers of the womb: the dome sky, which the queens of the universe made to keep out Saturn's moons;

Pangaea, which became Middle-Earth; and the abyss under the earth, the great underworld.

DOME SKY MIDDLE-EARTH ABYSS

The dome was made up of liquid glass, which separated the sea in the sky from the abyssal sea beneath Middle-Earth; there were the seraphim, also known as the Van Allen belts, which guarded the corona of the heavens. Two black women, the seraphim, didn't allow anyone in or out of the dome above the skies; in the abyss, two cherubic black women guarded the entrance of the portal that led to the skies from the ocean abyss. Spaceships didn't come from the skies; they came out of the abyss There were many cities on the moon and sun; melanated humans came from the sun, and pale mankind came from the moon. They didn't have a soul from the morning star or sun. Their soul was from the death star, or moon; the sun was positive, and the moon was negative. This is where the concept of God and the devil comes from.

The queen mom told us the planet, or Middle-Earth, wasn't a round sphere. It was a flat plane. The upper level was the horn of Africa; the middle level was the Americas; the bottom level was Europe. The queen told us Middle-Earth didn't turn; it was the sky that was moving. God was personified as the feminine the Holy Trinity was the father, sky; the mother, sea; and the child, Middle-Earth. The Saturn moon was the most important luminaire for the life-forms on Middle-Earth to be observed because it gave us signs and information Saturn used to communicate with mankind and reptilian. The moon was also a weapon that the reptilians used to punish those who broke the law on Saturn. One of the many miseducations of mankind was that the sun and the moon were bigger than Middle-Earth. The queen of the universe created the sun, and Saturn created the moon. Both were much smaller than the earth; both of them were the same size. The sun and the moon were two black balls that illuminated. The sun was the representation of life, and the moon was the representation of death. Life and death both were just star gates into different realms. Everything mankind taught under the construct of education and civilization, both were weapons of misinformation and programs that connected to other conduits of control. We believed that humans were under the spell of these systems and that older programs such as religion and history were artificial narratives that were seared into the minds and hearts of human beings. Only the queens of the universe, using the sun, could remove this powerful curse. Saturn's moon placed with the gift of knowledge of self human slavery and nearly brought about the permanent mental estate of Tartarus. *Tartarus* is a Greek word meaning "mental prison," a never-ending journey of mystery and illusions in one's head— eternal damnation. This concept of divine punishment and torment was also known as the bottomless pit; without the ritual of illumination, enlightenment wouldn't penetrate the dark grave of Tartarus. This mental prison state of the mind, Tartarus, had been described as a formless planet—waste and void. Darkness reigned day and night, and the people wandered for eternity, dumb, dead, and blind. Once the rings were placed on Saturn by the queens of the universe and renamed Tartarus, the collector of souls, with the term signed to your soul to the devil, came from reptilians, creating agents for Saturn. I was only a cub, but the stories the queen mom told us were amazing; all of the wisdom and knowledge of the clan was passed down through the females. The deluge put out the fires, the flooding caused the river to crest, and the herds were starting to show up—first the buffalos, then the roan antelopes and reedbucks. It was a family affair. The lions didn't control Dinknesh, Ethiopia. It was one of about eight countries where the hyena was the top hunter; we went through training (like school) daily; the females were the instructors and the best hunters. Helen was the queen's right paw; her daughter Holly and I were best buddies; we were royalty, but fun and adventure came first. Holly had more responsibility than I did; she was probably going to be the next queen. The males spent 90 percent of our time training on security and protection for the clan. The females spent most of their time learning vibrational frequencies and hunting techniques. As the queen matriarch's son, my role was very different in the clan; my place in the clan was to be ceremonial, like a role model or idiomatic expression to keep the males motivated and maintaining proper supervision.

THE COMING-OF-AGE HOLLY

I was coming of age and able to hunt. The herds settled down near Bahir Gojjam, also known as Lake Tana, the beginning of the Blue Nile. The river was where the queens of the universe came to visit Middle-Earth in the form of a woman riding on a Walia ibex. Dinknesh was also known as Ethiopia, taking from the Greek letters. Cush was the birthplace of human beings; the queens of the universe set up a special place for the original human beings called the Nile Valley civilization. The queens of the universe visited the Nile Valley four times a year during the age of the pyramids; before Ethiopia, Egypt, and the Sudan, there was the Nile Valley civilization.

Black people of chemistry were the Kemetic people, the Nubian people, and the Cushite people; the Nile Valley civilization became the Abyssinian people, African Americans, the Sudanese, and most of the nations from the transatlantic slave trade. I wanted to play with Holly every day, but her role was changing. The queen and Helen were grooming her to become the next queen. What I didn't know was that the queen and Helen were planning something for the clan. Holly took me for a walk in our usual childhood place. I grabbed a tree branch and waited for Holly to bite the other end; we always played tug-of-war. She initiated a very different conversation than what I was used to. Holly wasn't in the mood for playing; she said that we needed to think about growing up. I started worrying this next-queen business was going to Holly's head. Holly said, "I didn't come here to play. I came to start a family." I didn't understand. She said, "I brought you here to start a family with me." Helen, Holly's mom, and the queen, my mom, had planned for us to connect and become soul mates, so Holly got in the position of love. She said, "Perform your duty." We lay down together. This was a part of my ceremonial responsibility. I had to accept, and Holly moved beyond the sphere of her den duties and children to the throne. The queen would stay in power until the prime of her life was finished; by that time she would have trained Holly with the history and laws of the clan. Our queen was very powerful chronologically. She was in her prime. She gave her gifts of wisdom evenly to the clan. Mom was all about sacrifice and hard work. The queen chose to be independent of her pleasures and satisfaction; her instincts and creative impulses embodied the clan.

HOLLY, QUEEN HELEN, AND THE QUEEN'S PLAN

Holly and I started to spend more time together as a family. Our relationship changed for the better. I was one of the most respected males in the clan, but the lowest of the females had more power. The queen and Helen were notorious for changing the rules of the clan, but they made sure the power was never challenged between males and females. The queen called everyone into the den for story time; this was the queen's way of teaching us about Pangaea and Middle-Earth. The queen told us about the firmament, this vast solid dome created by the queens of the universe in the second age to divide the primal sea into upper and lower portions so that the dry land could appear, called Pangaea. She—being God—divided the water from the waters, so the sky was blue because of the ocean above our head; the dome was made up of part of metal moon rock and fire. The firmament or expanse was the atmosphere of Pangaea, where the birds and clouds were, and the sun and the star were placed before Saturn added the moon. The firmament had many levels. The thermosphere was where mankind created its space station to produce photoionization; the mesosphere was the defense system to protect against meteors; the stratosphere was where the ozone layer began; the troposphere was where the transmitting of radio signals bounced from; the exosphere was where the satellites and spaceship hovered; the ionosphere was the active part of the atmosphere that allowed the eyes to behold colors and depended on the sun's energy to grow the aurora. The aurora was sometimes referred to as the polar lights; these northern and southern lights over the sky of Pangaea played a unique role in what the naked eye saw.

AURORA ATMOSPHERE FIRMAMENT

The queen told us that the only truth in the Bible was that animals were here before humans and mankind; the plant and animal kingdoms knew all the secrets of Pangaea and Middle-Earth. There was a time when animals and plants had shared the planet alone; humans had come out of the abyss and settled on Pangaea, now Middle-Earth. The ocean was the womb of life—that's why humans are 70 percent water and electricity. When you look up in the sky, it's hard to tell if anything is going on up there. Our queen was preparing the clan for the peaceful transfer of power; the queen had built a reputation in East Africa. She had made it possible for other territories to control large landscapes and push lions out. Later that night, before we went to sleep, she felt grieved in her spirit because the blood moon was coming. Our queen was different. Most clans hurt on the blood moon. It was forbidden to hunt on Pangaea, now Middle-Earth, during a blood moon. The queen and Helen were honored; they felt that that was why the queens of the universe loved our clan. After the queen went to sleep, I walked the grounds in the back of the den thinking about everything from Holly becoming the queen to her pregnancy. A group of lions attacked the den and tried to run the clan away. They had underestimated our clan; we were the strongest, most skilled clan in the horn of Africa. Five lions attacked three females and two males while most of us were sleeping.

The clan overwhelmed them in a tight spot. One of the males grabbed the queen. I heard the commotion and pushed my way straight to the queen. Out of fear, the clan froze. Helen was in a fast and deadly fight with a lioness, and Holly was trying to get the lioness off her mother. I wasn't sure what to do, so I closed my eyes and grabbed the lion holding the queen by the testicles; he let her go in pain. The other lions took off after seeing their leader in pain. The lion's name was Lexus. I brought him down to the ground. We all gave him a beating to remember. The queen demanded that that was enough. The lion had very little life in his body, and I went for his neck. I could feel the bones crushing. The entire clan stopped as the queen requested I kill Lexus that night. Helen and Holly watched as I defied the queen's orders. The males attacked and dragged his body out of the den; the rain fell that night hard. Nobody slept. Helen was hurt bad, but she was going to be fine, and the queen was hurt but was expected to heal just fine. Word spread throughout all the lion prides in Africa about the death of Lexus, and the hyena clans, for the first time, were united. All the males were chanting my name, Horus. I became a general overnight with the respect of all the clans' males; this worried the respective queens in each clan because no male had ever wielded this kind of power. The next morning I went for a walk, and word was sent to me that

Holly had just given birth to my son. We rushed back to the den. When I saw him, my heart was full of joy and love. I named him Heru. Holly and Heru were all I could ask for. The queens of the universe had blessed me and our clan. Once Holly became the queen, the clan would continue to progress after Mom stepped down. I was approached by different clans to chase the lions out of Ethiopia once and for all. I needed promises from the queen. I had males and females backing me. I went before the queen to get her blessings on the mission; she refused and gave me a warning. The queens of the sister clans thought I had too much power. The army kept growing until the queens of our sister clans got together and had a meeting; they finally gave the go-ahead after deep thought. I led the army into Ras Dashen; there were only eight lions in all of Abyssinia. I gave the order to charge the lions; they saw the numbers of the clan put together; they didn't even put up a fight and fled immediately. We chased the lions into Kenya; for the first time, we didn't have any lions in Abyssinia. The queen wasn't happy—she knew the lions would want revenge. For the first time in an age, all the clans were at peace; all the queens of the sister clans in Abyssinia needed me to assure them that my influence over the clans would translate into an uprising. With all the celebrating and mingling between clans, I didn't notice the blood moon until later that night, when everybody was in the den listening to the queen's story.

BLOOD MOON LIONS ABYSSINIA

The sister clans were out hunting during the blood moon. The queen didn't allow anyone in our clan to leave the den until the blood moon of Saturn was over. It was very nice spending time together; we had food to last us two days. My son, Heru, was growing so fast; Holly didn't let him out of her sight. I was Heru's size when Holly and I used to play; now, seeing her as a mother, it was a very interesting feeling. Abyssinia felt very different; with the lions gone, the herds worried the Hyena clans would kill more. The foxes and wolves supported this decision; this was an opportunity for them. We didn't have to hurt so early anymore because the lions were gone. The queen told us that what had happened was because of the blood moon. There are many moons—ten colors of the moon. The blood-red moon was the most dangerous for land. The blue moon controlled the sea and the waters; the blue moon came four times in an age, every 505 years. The blue moon also controlled the skies with frequencies and chemicals that the reptilians sprayed. Then there was the silver moon; it was a calendar timer for mankind on Middle-Earth. The story of the devil dancing in the pale moonlight had started two and a half ages ago; the pale silver moon was a reminder to mankind their time was almost up. The green moon was for control over land and all plant life in the rain forest; the trees talked to one another. The green moon came twice in an age, every 1,010 years. During the purple moon, the reptilians walked Middle-Earth and warred with the women on the abyss floor. On the bottom of the water, there were black-and-white lines; they warred on that trail. The orange moon was for control over the feminine creations; it was a reminder that all males came from females and that the truth must be kept a secret. Pangaea was feminine; the soil was the womb and gave birth to all seeds. The queens of the universe visited Abyssinia ten times an age, every 202 years. The orange moon came, and it was the only time the Walia ibex's eyes glowed orange. I can't forget perhaps the most important one of them all, the black moon. It called the holy sea like Rome, the only time it was seen during the war between the sun and moon. The black moon was the human's moon; its color was originally black and a sign to mankind of the alpha and omega. Many assumed the moon was pale because it illuminated. Ages ago the moon used to land in the Arctic for thirty days; during that time, the sun didn't show up for thirty days. In Europe the moon traveled through twelve gates in the sky; each gate was a portal of energy. Twelve hours of night recharged the carbon-based life-form. The moon was a hollowed-out planetoid; there was no doubt the entire solar system had been engineered by an entity with consummate technological prowess, the queens of the universe, but the moon had been engineered from a different source on Saturn. I lay in front of the den that night watching the blood moon. Helen and the queen were still healing from the attack by the lions, so the time off from hunting, in this case, was good. Holly came out to join me; the queen told us that the blood moon stood for death and judgment but that to us, it meant love. The queen was getting older and becoming sickly. She was planning to name Holly queen one year ahead of time. She sent for me to come into her private quarters in the back of the den. Helen and the queen had just finished up a meeting with all the females of the clan. The queen asked to be alone; everyone took their leave. "My son, your life is in danger. You are not to leave this den until I can get an agreement with the queens from our sister clans. Word has come to me they believe you're planning to change our tradition.

The males in their clans started to rebel in your name. Maybe you can talk to them. My son, we don't need a war between our clans. The wolves and foxes are growing stronger, and so are the wild dogs; it's only a matter of time before the lions try to return." The queen told me she had decided to step down after the blood moon. "Arrangements have already been made. Helen is preparing Holly, my son," Mom said. "I am sick and dying." The queen said, "The blood moon was a sign." Shaking my head in disbelief, I ran out of the den and down to the Blue Nile. My mother's leadership was all the clan had. She was the wisest of all the queens and the oldest. Life suddenly turned upside down for me. I lay near the Nile thinking and asking the queens of the universe to heal the queen mom for our clan. My tears just fell into the Nile. I wanted to curse that blood moon of Saturn; just before I could curse the moon, a woman's image approached me. She spoke my vibrational frequency. Next to her stood a Walia ibex. This Walia was all black with glowing orange eyes.

The woman asked me, "Why do you weep?" I remembered the stories the queen mom had told us about the queens of the universe. Whoever this woman was, the divine energy was all over the ground; it felt like the sun was under me. I asked the woman to spare my mother's life and take mine instead. She climbed on the Walia and walked into the Blue Nile slowly.

I begged, "Please take me—please." She kept going.

Just before her head went underneath the Nile, she said, "I am the eastern oracle."

EAST ORACLE QUEEN STEP DOWN

That creeped me out enough to run back to the den; on the way back, a sister clan was patrolling the area, six females and four males. I didn't know there was a warrant out for me from three sister clans. The princess of the clan was present and invited me to come back to answer for the charges; she gave me her word I would be safe and receive a fair trial. The females surrounded me with smiles on their faces. I asked for safe passage to my clan, and the princess refused. Two of the males challenged the princess of the sister clan; when the other two males figured out who I was, they sided with the other two who were standing with me. We were in a stalemate, so the princess granted me passage. She had no choice. This was the problem: the females didn't have the same full control that they once had. Once I made it back to the den, the queen placed me on a restricted watch. Helen instructed all the clans that I was not to leave the den for two weeks. The queen needed some time to talk with the sister clans. The clans were divided. All the males supported the vindication of my name, and half the females supported my innocents. The clans knew this was all politics. The leadership structure felt threatened, but the males having a paragon was a positive thing. I never asked for this. It had all started when I killed Lexus and chased the lions out of Abyssinia. I just protected my queen and clan—being a hero wasn't on my mind. The queen was planning to make a deal with the sister clans and bring me before them to explain this was a misunderstanding. My action of killing the lion was to protect the queen; as ridiculous as it sounds, the females' order of things takes this seriously—any male trying to disrupt the power structure can be put to death. The queen was very sickly. She was growing weaker by the day. Our sister clans knew this, so the queen sent Helen to bring the peace treaty. Every day that went by, the queen's eyesight was weening, so on the second night of the blood moon, the ceremony of the coronation took place. Holly was made queen. The crowning of a sovereign by law must be given thirty days without any conflict of sister clans. The queen gathered the clan together for her last story as queen. She told us about the power of the Blue Nile and the women who kept the sea in order.

There were millions of mermaids in the sea. They decorated the oceans; they added all the flowers and pearls; they were the most beautiful creatures ever made. As females, their skin was black as the Nile. At night, with a voice that could put any male under a spell, some wore braids, lox, and afros. Ages ago they had been called sirens because of their voices. Pirates hadn't stood a chance. During the second age, the pirates would deep-dive looking for treasure; the sirens would protect the treasure for the enslaved humans to return to them once they were freed. All carbon-based life-forms were produced from the abyss, crafted by the hands of women. During the last three days of October, near the mouth of the Blue Nile, after midnight there was a chorus of women's voices vibrating off the water. Their voices could be heard for miles away, and the water mysteriously changed to light blue at night for one hour—you could see straight to the bottom. The woman riding the Walia ibex cleaned the earth from the blood moon; she had the power to reverse death; some said she was God herself. This was the last night of the blood moon, so many things had happened in two days. The morale of the clan was low. Everyone knew the queen was sick. The queen had called the clan to come close to her. She made the clan swear to honor and respect our new queen. She gave Holly a week to prepare her for the transfer of power. Our sister clans sent word to Helen that out of respect for the queen's sickness, they would drop the charges and false claims against me. Even though Holly would be queen, her mother, Helen, would be the queen's trusted adviser. Helen would be running the clan until Holly learned to grow into her role. This news of the other clans' decision to end the conflict came at the perfect time. The queen felt peace and tranquility. Helen played a big role in stabilizing the clan. She carried the army of females' loyalty. Early the next morning, Helen, Holly the queen, and I watched the horizon. My son stayed asleep normally until high noon. I still had faith in the queen's recovery. She had been the cornerstone of our clan and all Abyssinia. She was the centerpiece we all looked to for guidance. The horizon was so beautiful that morning that the queen made time to spend alone with Holly. She'd groomed her for many months now; it was time to share the secrets only passed down through the matriarch. I could tell this was a challenge for Holly, to watch the queen dying with an illness that we couldn't cure. The clan was very happy with the queen's choice. Everyone felt at ease. The last thing we needed was strife between the clans. Helen made a celebration for the queen and Holly; delegations from sister clans were invited. The queen's energy was returning to her slowly. Helen and I were the first to notice. Both Helen and I were going to play a big role in Holly's royal reign. Holly had great support from her mother. Helen had spent her whole life in the queen's service. I, on the other paw, had the overwhelming support of the males in all Abyssinia.

HELEN, HOLLY QUEEN REUNION CLAN

The blood moon had passed. There was peace once again. The queen was alive. My wife was the next queen, and my son was healthy—not bad for an immigrant. While everybody was enjoying themselves, I kept thinking about the woman riding the Walia who went into the Nile. I wanted to share what happened with my wife or the queen, but it was hard to find the time. I didn't want to make the moment about me despite the fact this could have a prophetic meaning. I wanted the queen to interpret my experience. Normally the females had the celestial encounters. It was offensive and sacrilege. One could argue this is what had gotten me into the mess I had just gotten out of. In our culture, males had a small role to play in any decision-making. Sixty percent of us loved it that way—all we had to do was eat, sleep, and shit. I had meant well in defending the queen. I had killed a lion. The problem was I didn't have the promise that was taking as a power grab. Dusk couldn't be better. The night was getting underway. Our unity was necessary to maintain control and keep the lions out as the night took full control of the constellation. The stars add to the ambience. The moon was unusually large and more deceptively beautiful than the night before. Our queen left earlier than the rest of us young folks. She needed her rest. She didn't want to overdo it. Helen took Heru to the den. It was past his bedtime. Holly and I took a little walk. We both wanted to spend time alone. It came naturally. I told Holly, "My African queen, I love you with all my heart.

She said, "My African king, I love you more." We spent the night together away from the den. The next morning, Helen and the queen weren't exactly thrilled about our disappearing act; at the same time, they were very happy. Holly and I were supposed to lead the horizon hunt. The early bird indicated the worm was out later. We started late. The hardest thing about hunting late was that the sun made things difficult.

Helen and the queen spoke to us both; they said at the same time, "You kids can't expect to lead a clan if they don't know where you are."

"Rule number one: a queen never goes anywhere without a member of her royal court. My son, you're going to have to get used to your wife being the queen. I never go anywhere without two female escorts or at least Helen. Even when with your husband, Holly, you must be accompanied by a royal escort." The queen went on to say, "The clan and all of our sister clans will be watching you. Being the queen is a permanent responsibility, and, Horus, you're going to have to help make things easier for her. This is why when the new queen is crowned, it usually takes up to three months before she can obtain her full power. Holly is going to make an awesome queen, and I'm going to support her." I joined the clan, which was already hunting on the Nile. Holly went back to the den to be by the queen's side. Every moment was crucial because the queen didn't have much time to groom Holly. Helen's dream had come true for her daughter; she had carefully raised her in the royal state of mind to compete for the queen's heart. There were four other females the queen had been looking over as potentials. The clan returned from a successful hunt to the den. The queen sent for me. She was taking her last breath. The sickness had come back even worse. I couldn't stand to see her like this. She had helped every member of our clan, and none of us could help her when she's in need. I needed to clear my mind, so I left the den. Holly ran after me, demanding an escort accompany me, but I needed to be alone. There wasn't any reason for me to fear. The lions were gone, and all the clans were at peace. The sound of the Nile River could heal the pain of the heart. My childhood flashed before my eyes. Our leader, the queen, was my mother first; this felt like a double-edged sword. I just wasn't ready for her to go. A female from a sister clan approached me to say the queen had sent for me; it was time for me to face my pain and support Holly and comfort the queen. On my way back to the den, the female who had come to get me fell in a shallow hole; she couldn't feel her right leg, so I helped her out of the hole. I smelled lions close by. The moment I looked up, two male lions jumped on me. It had been a setup. The female hyena had carried out the orders of her queen, Harriet. I didn't even feel the pain. It happened so fast. The female was sent to inform my clan that the lions had returned and killed me by the Nile, and by the time my clan got there to help it was too late. I faded to black. My eyes were closed; my body, mutilated. Then I saw a blue light and heard the sound of water. My eyes were too heavy to open.

And I heard her voice say, "I am the eastern oracle. Do you choose to live or give life to the queen?" My decision wasn't easy because of my son and Holly, but I chose my mother. The queen's health returned to her immediately, and the clan mourned my death for weeks. I didn't get a chance to say goodbye, but I did visit the den one last time when the queen was telling a story—

just a flash of my image standing next to the queen. Most of the clan saw me and became afraid, but the queen, Holly, was at peace. And I was grateful to the eastern oracle for giving me that opportunity. I woke up in the bedroom with an awful headache. The time on the VCR was still 4:44. Slowly my memory came back to me; every minute was painful.

I went right back to the map. The hyena and penguin were missing; with every minute that went by, I realized my family was gone.

HYENA SOUTHERN ORACLE LIONS

I had to force myself to continue to move forward on the map. I took the polar bear and rolled the dice; the bottom of the polar bear read, "North Pole." My room turned black and cold in the blink of an eye. Just like that, I was in the arctic with Polly, my cutie polar bear cub. I was teaching her how to catch and eat salmon. The technique is to walk along the rocks perfectly and listen to the changing sound of the water. Polly had to learn fast. I would have to leave her alone soon and start a new breeding cycle. Polly was almost three and still hadn't mastered her smells. Tomorrow I planned on leaving Polly. That was the only way she was going to survive the wolves who were waiting until I left—they'd been following us for three days. The water, along with Polly's instincts, would have to protect Polly now. The most important smell was the wolves. I created for Polly a day den and an enclosed den. Our family had first started in the Russian arctic and migrated all over the arctic circle. I was born on Wrangel Island off the East Siberian Sea, thirteen thousand square kilometers of the most beautiful ice structures. Polly had been born between the Bering Strait, closer to Alaska. Wrangel Island was special; it was the only island we had to ourselves. My mother was born on Cape Blossom, the place I had learned to survive. We had shared the island with our neighbors the walruses on Wrangel Island when the ice melted and the water rose. I remembered those were the best times. Our family had stayed together and bonded. My father was born off of the US coast, in a place called Prudhoe Bay. The hardest place to hunt had always been Greenland, the place I met Polly's father off of the coast of Nord. I was making my way to Norway, a place called Longyearbyen. Polly wasn't strong enough to make the trip. This time of the year, all the walruses were gathering there. My father used to tell us stories of when dragons ruled the arctic circle. Dad had told us that some of the dragons had walked on two legs and talked just like humans. Dragons then were known as dinosaurs. Mankind suggested that the ice age had killed them. This simply wasn't true. The dragons had gone underground. Papa had noticed a different kind of dragon, the reptilian dinosaur. The reptilian resembled a human; it wore clothes and used weapons identical to humans. The reptilians built houses and made devices for communication. The dragon was the same as the dinosaur; it was only during the third age of mankind that the term *dinosaur* had been coined. For two of the last three ages that mankind had been on Middle-Earth, the dragons had helped mankind to establish control over humans during the start of the third age of mankind on Middle-Earth. The reptilians had been forced to go back to the moon. This hollowed planetoid was no longer allowed to land on Pangaea. The reptilians had built spacecrafts for mankind to visit the moon to receive technology and instructions. The moon sent transmissions to Pangaea; it was a satellite. The moon disk hadn't always been in the sky. The elder said it had come during the first age of mankind on Middle-Earth. The reptilians used to land the moon in the arctic for months at a time. The dragons were so known as the dinosaurs had died because of the moon. The moon controlled time, and the effect of the moonlight lengthened the dragons' life span. During the third age of mankind on Middle-Earth, the queens of the universe had held the sun in place over the arctic for months. The moon had malfunctioned and overheated, causing it not to rise during the summer months. The radiator inside the moon had overheated; the moon had been grounded for years. The dragons or dinosaurs had died in one year. The climate had destroyed them. The moon landing had been very important to the polar bears. The moon had brought life from all around the world to the arctic; the lack of the moon's orbit had caused the sun to stand still over Egypt, freezing three-quarters of the planet, killing the dragons.

DRAGON MOON LANDING

Early the next morning, while Polly was sleeping, the mother in me was planning. I went hunting. Polly needed every bit of help I could give her to survive. Polly had more time with me than most cubs get with their mothers. Polly still didn't perceive what was about to happen. I brought food back to the den and left shortly after—my journey had to continue. Just like that, Polly was on her own; the ice returned to the island. I left to start my new breeding cycle. I had so many memories of Wrangel Island that getting stuck on the island could be life or death. Polly had gotten so used to the island that she couldn't part with the land. Nights in the arctic were more beautiful than anywhere in the world. The moon landing had contributed to the survival of life in the arctic. The moon landed in the arctic and drew life close to it. Hundreds of fish and sea lions came out of the ocean; even wolves fell in love with the moon. I set out on my journey toward the deep parts of the arctic circle near Scandinavia. This time of year, food sources were plentiful. Polly wasn't strong enough to make the trip, but she knew her way around here and Russia. I told Polly to head for Pevek—close to the island off the mainland—Uelen in Russia, and Nome in the United States. She'd be able to survive off the fish; all the walrus, penguins, and sea lions gathered there for safety. If I was going to be successful for my next breeding cycle, I would need heavier meals. The stars traveled on the outside of the Arctic cycle. The stars were easy to follow. There were only forty stars in the entire sky; they traveled with the moon as an escort in a circle. The sun and moon circle our flat disk, Middle-Earth; it was easy to navigate my way because the sky was moving, not the planet. The arctic was so beautiful because the moonlight shone off the ice; the ambience was more amazing than Egypt. The arctic had a form of daylight at night. On my way toward Scandinavia, I found a cub that was lost without its mother and hungry. The cub followed me. I believed the poor young thing to be at least one and a half years old. Our vibrational frequency and hearing were all we had to survive, and the cub didn't have either. On top of that, its sense of smell hadn't grown since the cub was born. This meant its mother had probably died or left early; most moms tried to leave at least by the age of two, giving the cub time to develop its senses. Polly was on my mind. I gave her the best opportunity possible to survive. The cub started following others on the journey toward Scandinavia. I didn't have any regrets, but there was always a little guilt.

My life started when my parent's life ended. That was when everything I learned kicked in and life began. I was sure Polly would agree. One day we would meet up again and watch the stars together. After nearly six days of travel, I stopped to take a break near Novaya Zemlya, to rest up for the final push toward Scandinavia. I was very hungry and needed to stop to feed, but I could smell a pack of wolves on my trail; they were getting closer. I heard the alpha female call the wolves away to much easier prey. After spending many years as neighbors, I had learned almost all their vibrational frequencies. The biggest predator to the polar bear was mankind, who had lived among us for three ages. It was the only way they could avoid the sun, adding melanin to their skin. Without the arctic circle, white supremacy couldn't exist. The Holy Grail of mankind was the law of the arctic circle; the arctic circle was all the proof one needed to understand the flat earth. This was the very reason only mankind controlled the arctic circle, also known as the ends of the earth. The entire outer Pangaea was surrounded by an ice wall with subzero temperatures so low that mankind wasn't allowed to venture in. Middle-Earth had four equal parts unknown to mankind (this is where the term *boundaries of fantasia* comes from), which had eventually become the four winds of the earth held by angels. The first boundary was the firmament, a large hemispherical roof guarded by a woman named Domus. The second boundary was the abyss, the underworld in the sea guarded by a woman named Abysmal-Sheol; some said the gates of Sheol were in the Bermuda Triangle, and it was hell to pay to enter. The third boundary was the ice walls, also known as the pearly gates, guarded by a woman named Glacies-Petram. Legend said her eyes were made of hot ice and one look at her could freeze any fleshly being in a moment. The fourth boundary was the Lehmann discontinuity, understood to be the middle of the land; this was where the most pressure metals were found and guarded by a woman named Kora-Ember.

THE FOUR BOUNDARIES

The arctic circle was called the Pentagon at the beginning of the dark age because it connected mankind from Canada, America, Europe, Greenland, and Asia. The arctic circle, more importantly, is where all the animal kingdoms would come together to hold a conference; they were the real caretakers that kept the sky, sea, and land clean. All animals had a vested interest in Pangaea and cleaning up the mess mankind made. Pangaea belonged to us all, especially the arctic circle. It was the only home polar bears knew. There was a trail we called the polo grounds; polar bears followed this path and left vital information behind. The oldest polar bear was always on the trail passing out information for a small fee. Many travelers gave birth on the polo grounds. There were tens of millions of footprints from our ancestors. Papa Polar ran a very large operation; the fees he charged were to pay the sigils to spy on the walrus. I needed at least three fishes to pay from for knowledge. I needed to know the best breeding place this time of year and where the walruses were heading. Papa Polar paid young polar bears and sigils to gather this data. Lucky for me, I was able to catch four fish. Papa Polar said I needed to head toward Spitsbergen, Svalbard, off the Norwegian Sea; the walruses would be there in two days, and there was a caravan of mankind down there filming. Papa Polar was also a matchmaker; he knew the good males from the crazy bulls. The polo grounds had been around for at least five ages. Papa Polar's family had been selling and collecting information on every polar bear in the arctic circle; the polo grounds were most important for young cubs separated from their mother. I had been to Spitsbergen, Svalbard, before; it was a beautiful place mixed with ice and exotic plant life near the Fugelsongen, high up in the arctic. Spitsbergen, Svalbard, was a very competitive place; there were reindeer and blue whales, but most of all, perhaps the most dangerous of them was mankind filming and hunting. The only man to live in peace on the land was a man by the name of Kris Kringle—a very strange man. Papa Polar always shared stories about old Kris Kringle; they said he lived with the reindeer. Kris Kringle wasn't welcome among his people; whenever he would come to town, people would say, "Run! Kris Kringle—Krampus—is coming." Krampus was a nickname the villagers had given him. Kris Kringle was a carpenter who made antique furniture for all of Europe. The story went that a curse had been placed on him by the king of England. On every full moon, the story said that Kris Kringle turned into Krampus, a hideous monster. The king of England had learned that Kris Kringle had a secret relationship with the king's daughter Elizabeth. The story went that he had been the most handsome of all mankind, with deep-blue eyes that glowed when he laughed. Elizabeth had run away with Kris many times and had a child with him. The king had ordered his men to find Kris and put him in prison for life, and they had. While Kris was awaiting trial, the king had paid the court to rule a sentence of death by hanging. News about Kris Kringle and Elizabeth had spread all over the world; his father, Christopher Nicholas Kringle, was a great builder and helped fund the Knights Templar. Christopher Nicholas Kringle was an architectural legend; they said he had helped to build the many cathedrals in Rome and Greece and was the great-great-grandson of King Solomon. The cathedrals Christopher built were in honor of the king of Rome's wife Catherine the Great, whose granddaughter Catherine III of Russia continued the tradition of building cathedrals with the help of Christopher's son Kris Kringle. Papa Polar told us Christopher Nicholas Kringle was special and related to Jesus Christ—that's why the king of Rome created Christmas on December 25, to honor both Jesus Christ and Christopher Nicholas Kringle. The cathedrals were used to hold celebrations of the birth of Jesus and the architect of the cathedrals, so the king made Nicholas a saint. Papa Polar said Christopher was special because he was blessed with long life from his bloodline of the Dunedain family and he was nearly 444 years old when he died. The Dunedain could just be a myth, but Papa Polar said they were part man and part reptilian. This is all speculation, if you ask me. Papa Polar was just telling stories to pass the time. Papa Polar said once the courts ruled death by hanging for Kris Kringle, Elizabeth sent word to Rome that the son of Saint Nicholas was in trouble. Rome ordered his release, and the very next day he was set free. The people would never leave him alone, so Kris Kringle and Elizabeth changed their names to Mrs. and Mrs. Claus. The only way they could be together was to run away, and that they did, to the North Pole, and they were never again seen in public. Kris and Elizabeth were known as Mrs. and Mrs. Claus; they continued the work of building furniture, so Elizabeth, Mrs. Claus, came up with the idea of making toys for children to help change the image of Kris and Mrs. Claus. Every year on Christmas, December 25, Mr. and Mrs. Claus honored the celebration of the day made by the king of Rome to his father, Christopher Nicholas Kringle. The arctic circle is filled with many rich histories and stories; this just happens to be one of my favorites because of the happy ending.

MR. AND MRS. CLAUS, SPITSBERGEN, SVALBARD

It was now time for me to make my way to Spitsbergen, Svalbard. I started at dawn. Papa Polar said it was very important to only travel during the cover of night to avoid mankind. A few hours into my journey, I could hear the cry of a polar cub; it was coming from a nearby house with smoke coming from the roof. I wasn't going to stop, but the mother in me wanted to help; the cub was caught in a rope—some sort of trap that was covered up by snow. This is why cubs should travel without their mother; the poor thing probably smelled food coming from the house. I started chewing through the rope and tried to keep the cub quiet and calm at the same time so I could free him. I was almost done until the lights in the house came on. The cub then started making noise, so I ran to hide behind a small hill near the house; two men came out, one with a large stick and the other with a rifle. They started beating the cub to get him to flee, but his foot was caught in the rope; I could see the blood dripping on the ice, and the cub kept fighting, and they kept beating him. I ran toward them to scare them away so I could free him, and they fired two shots, and both of them hit me; my anger didn't let me feel the pain. The men ran back into the house, and I freed the cub; the both of us ran far away from the house before we stopped to catch our breath. The cub was fine and stayed with me the rest of the night, cold and frightened; he slept like my baby under me. I slept for a moment and was awakened by the voice of a woman who spoke in my vibrational frequency; she kept saying, "Your mother is waiting for you." I assumed she had found the cub's mother, but the cub was gone, and she repeated, "Your mother is waiting for you." I couldn't stand up fully, but I could see my body lying on the ice. Then she said, "I am the northern oracle." She was a beautiful black woman with a large afro and lightning coming from her hair; she said to me, "Go in peace." I died that night and never made it to Spitsbergen, Svalbard. In the dark I could hear people talking and the sound of a woman yelling.

NORTHERN ORACLE

At Mount Sinai Beth Israel hospital in North America, on October 28, 1980, at approximately 4:44 a.m., I was born to a beautiful black woman. I smiled at her. I was quickly taken away from her to another room in the hospital; on my way there, I could hear Frank Sinatra somewhere beyond the sea playing in the corridor. My birth from my mothership to the birth of the state began; a certificate was created as a bond or note of purchase the local government gave to my mother, along with authorization to work as a security of social engineering, a card with nine numbers on it. If you haven't guessed already, I'm not your average bear from Jellystone Park; the 1980s were influenced by neon colors and the expression of new age music. Music was used as a political state; disco, hip-hop, pop, rock, reggae, and jazz were a reflection of the creativity humans displayed after being physically freed from the slavery from mankind. Black people used music to change the face of slavery, like the gas in the vehicle music pushed the message of civil rights; slavery and oppression seemed like a thing of the past. Racism, the power of another race used to determine the destiny of another race, was placed on the back burner; international affairs had become more important than domestic subjugation. Television, a harmless-seeming device, captured the minds of the captured like a Rubik's Cube; black people were so entertained they forgot about their sovereignty. After years of insurrection, integration soon became the only option. Ronald Reagan, set to be the fortieth US president, was in the middle of a fierce debate against incumbent Jimmy Carter. October 28 was my day, but most of the black community was watching the debate; the black community had been a part of the Republican Party since Abraham Lincoln's Emancipation Proclamation. Mankind wasn't about to free the humans who had built their societies, so the Emancipation Proclamation provided a form of freedom; the debate didn't live up to the hype. Most of the nation was watching *Fantasy Island* or *Love Boat*; *Gilligan's Island* was still a big smash. The 1980s were all about Pink Floyd, whose eleventh album, *The Wall*, sold over thirty million copies; the only thing the box office needed to sell out movies in the theaters was simply two thumbs up from Siskel and Ebert. The Pittsburgh Steelers won the 1980 Super Bowl. Russia was the evil empire and boogeyman of the day, and the Soviet Union, a socialist republic, hosted the 1980 Olympics in Moscow. On March 2, 1980, for the second time in Florida's history, it snowed; the Gambino mobster John Gotti's crime family was running New York City. The biggest show in America was *Dallas*, and the million-dollar question was who shot JR. Eighty-three million people watched the episode that revealed the shooter. In 1980 America was introduced to Howard Stern, The Middle East had its share of problems: eight American soldiers died coming home from a mission in Iran. Magic Johnson's Lakers won the NBA championship. My grandmother loved *The Dukes of Hazzard*, a huge show in the eighties; everybody wanted a race car. *Pac-Man* was the biggest game of 1980; all the adults played for money. Nineteen eighty was also the beginning of the news network CNN; nobody noticed because the sequel to the movie *Star Wars*, *The Empire Strikes Back*, was on everybody's mind. With all the crazy things happening in the world, Richard Pryor still made us laugh even though his career was in serious jeopardy; the 1980s were filled with color. I'd like to think of black people's so-called freedom as a direct effect of the changes in American society; 1980 was the year of the independent woman, both black and white. The black community had experienced the control of the white man for over 360 years in America; people wanted a break from the past decades marked by riots, protest, race wars, division, and racial segregation. Dr.

Martin Luther King Jr.'s dream hadn't manifested in America yet; things like housing, health care, education, employment, and public transportation were still unequally administered. With the past of black people under an iron yoke still haunting the United States, the state of the union wasn't business as usual; 1980 brought with it a brave new generation with more opportunities. For the first time in America, black people's status changed, at least in public opinion. Rights and equality had become the sin of America from its original sin of slavery. The black community wanted equality in its homes, schools, and places of worship—and not just on television through sitcoms. Equality is a symbolic deed or expression; the white community assumed black people were satisfied with their token possessions and role in sport and entertainment. The white community came up with the idea of "making progress" with the black community, but after 400 years of slavery, making progress was a slap in the face. Just simply saying, "I thought we made progress, along with some domestic change" is like a person murdering his neighbor's entire family and naming his goldfish after them in memory of his neighbors. "We made progress" sadly came about because some basic services and utilities were finally made available in the black community. My father's side of the family lived in the state of Virginia in a small town called Chesapeake; in the commonwealth state, with its old English mind-set, many things hadn't changed since 1619. The transatlantic slave trade produced many famous tourist sites in Jamestown and all over Virginia and made money for the state, not the people affected by the tragedy. Just think of it: the people who did the slaving were receiving the proceeds and all rights reserved. What little wealth left over from the postslavery era that black people had accumulated was redistributed through the three branches of government: Congress, the executive branch, and the Supreme Court. I thought "we made progress" was an insult; the farmers and businesses—like the "Black Wall Street" financial districts that black people created for themselves—were destroyed by the local white supremacist terrorist groups. Essentially the black community was stripped down, but an apparatus comprised of the government, corporations, local patriots, and citizens' family reunions was created because slavery destroyed and disconnected black families all over the Americas; most of the records the government kept on the black community were sold to private banks and corporations. After 400 years of slavery, African American black families were rediscovering the world again; the black community had never had full access to the American dream— maybe because it was always only a dream. America was called the great experiment by the framers of the Constitution, and the black community was used as a lab rat; up until this day, every European nation has a stake in the fifty-state company called the United States. Many people believe it to be a country, not a company. Delaware versus Philadelphia was a secret hidden in plain sight to people under the veil of ignorance; the dark age was coming to an end; the age of enlightenment of the knowledge of self couldn't be more evident than in my generation. I remember on our way to church one morning, my mother and I took a taxi from Manhattan to the Brooklyn Tabernacle, and our taxi broke down on the Brooklyn Bridge, so we walked the rest of the way into Brooklyn. I gazed up at the bridge's architecture—a very impressive enormous structure. The lights were so bright, yet so many black people are ignorant to the fact we built the United States of America. I had an epiphany of my ancestors, thousands of them climbing the bridge out of the ocean, saying, "We built this country." This went on for about five minutes, but I'll remember it for a lifetime.

So I asked my mother who built America; she said, "Our ancestors, who were slaves." I didn't say another word that night; after church one of the members gave us a ride home. I became grown overnight, it seemed; it sounds worse than it looks, but I was a fatherless boy with a hard-working, strong black Christian mother. The streets raised most young black boys to be defensive toward black girls and offensive toward other black men; everyone is given a mission on their way to Middle-Earth. Blinded by the contraption most black people forget to search for their purpose but always feel a sense of déjà vu; our mission is hijacked at the womb by birth, an unlawful birth becomes the seizer of one's destiny using many methods. Medication, vaccines, and genetically modified organisms in our food, candy, and drinks rewire our molecular atoms; unattached chemicals cause malfunctions in our anatomy. The electrical charge in our water, fruits, and vegetables is replaced with poison, toxic materials, and hazardous waste; the body is like a computer being reprogrammed.

WELCOME TO THE SYSTEM PRE

Thirteen years later, in Brooklyn, New York, on October 22, 1993, a Friday night, I was sitting home bored. My mother was getting ready to go to a church service. It was a bit late, but I guess church in the black community is twenty-four hours.

Black woman are the main customers of the church; the very currency of the black church is the black woman. My older sister had plans of her own after my mother left. My baby sister and I usually were left alone; my older sister knew all my mother's business, which gave my older sister freedom, Keisha knew when my mother was planning to spend the night out at church praying. Having that information, she was able to schedule her childhood well. My younger sister and I wouldn't dare tell my mother that Keisha was leaving the house to hang out with her friends. The moment my mother left, so did Keisha; all Danielle and I required were some snacks. My baby sister and I would stay up watching movies all night. Danielle couldn't burn the midnight oil like me, which would lead to my snacking outside. The streets were very dangerous. Most people thought I was much older because of the friends I hung out with. My first adventure happened the moment my mother and Keisha left. I snuck out of the house normally, about two hours sometimes; I'd hang out until 2:00 a.m., just before my mother and sister returned. This night one of my friends, named Mice, suggested going to a house party a few blocks away; the party was free for girls and two dollars for boys. I wanted to go; it was only five minutes away, and I had never been to a house party before. But I did see the movie. Unfortunately, the party had moved to Yonkers, nearly two hours from Brooklyn. Untermyer Park, off the Hudson River in Westchester County, was bad news for I'd never been that far; there was no way I would risk it. The farthest I'd been on my own was the bookstore. I was hoping my friends would come up with different plans—something local. Mice spent nearly thirty minutes on a pay phone confirming the address;

plus, the word was that the boy-to-girl ratio was five girls to one boy. Once Mice hung up the phone, I could see in his eyes that we were going. He said Uncle Luke was performing with 2 Live Crew, and it was almost midnight. I was too embarrassed to tell them I couldn't go. Now the hard part was coming up with an excuse, I had a reputation to protect; for sure they would call me a wussy with four dollars in my pocket. The intelligent course of action would be to say good night, stop at the corner store, and get some snacks for me and Danielle. I had a crush on one of the girls in our crew. Yvette was sixteen, and we had kiss once on her fourteenth birthday. Yvette tried to persuade me to come to Yonkers, but it wasn't worth being grounded for five years and mouths of beatings. There were ten of us in the crew—six boys and four girls—and everybody wanted me to go. Everybody was dressed and ready to go except me. We were supposed to smoke a blunt and just kick it like we did every weekend, but Mice had come up with the suggestion of partying. Once we finished smoking, everybody started walking toward the subway station. Yvette was disappointed in me, and I walked home like a loser. I didn't stop at the store to get snacks for me and Danielle, which had been the plan two hours before. I went home so high I forgot the first door was locked. I climbed up the tree next to my room and went in through the window. My mother and Keisha hadn't returned yet, and Danielle was sleeping. I lay on my *Star Wars* bunk bed thinking about Yvette. Maybe my friends were out of my league. My friends' parents didn't mind them staying out all night as long as they stayed close, but my mother made me come home once the streetlights came on. This was like a scene from the movie *House Party*; this time I was the kid playing with fire. Curiosity started my vivid imagination thinking about all the beautiful natural-headed black girls dancing to "Doo Doo Brown" on the dance floor, sweating all over the place. Damn.

YONKERS 2 LIVE CREW SUBWAY

I snapped out of my vision. I heard a tap on my window. It was Yvette; she was throwing little pebbles at the window. She wanted to say goodnight. For the first time, she said, "I love you." For some reason I just said goodnight back and closed the window. The radio in my room was on WBLS. Bobby Brown's "Roni" was playing. I changed my clothes so fast. I got fly funky fresh with the smell goods I had stolen from a deacon in my church—some old-school-cologne vibes. I instantly became a product of my environment the ghetto life. I climbed out the window and ran so fast toward the subway, as if my life depended on it.

My heart was racing thinking about turning around; my good angel tried to convince me not to go, but my bad angel said, "Run faster—the night is yours." This time I listened to the bad angel. I arrived at the subway. I didn't see anybody.

The good angel said, "Go home."

The bad angel said, "Check downstairs." I went down the stairs on the subway platform; amazingly, Mice saw me before everyone else. I could tell by the smile on his face that he was happy to see me. My other friend Dice was trying to hook up with Yvette; when she saw me, her eyes lit up like two half dollars. She gave me a big hug and a kiss on the cheek. Some old-school dweeb had a boom box on the platform; he was jamming

Heavy D & the Boyz' "I Want Somebody for Me." The train was taking a very long time to come, giving me more time to think about going back home. At this point it was too late. Finally, the train came; there was no turning back now. The train ride went by so fast. We laughed and joked the entire way. We poked fun at everybody on the train. Mice lit a blunt in the middle of the train car; we all took turns smoking. The weed helped me forget about the consequences facing me when I got back home. The train ride to Yonkers took one hour and twenty minutes The Bronx felt like another state or country; there were so many different nationalities from South America, but they all seemed to be speaking Spanish. People said Yvette looked like Mary J. Blige; she was a very beautiful black girl, and she had a nice voice. Both of us had grown up in the black church and sang in the choir every Sunday morning. I had never been to a real party or a club. I had only been to baby showers and kids' birthday parties. Yvette and I kept making eye contact. I wasn't sure how our night was going to end, but something was brewing. We made it to the Bronx (East 241st Street, White Plain Road); we were still thirty minutes away, so we agreed to take a taxi, The taxi ride took only ten minutes. We pulled up to the location; the party was in a recreation center. So many black girls were standing in line to get into the party; everybody was wearing Cross Colours clothing, and all the females' hair was natural. I could hear MC Lyte's song "Ice Cream Dream" playing inside the party. I was ready to get inside, but we decided to stop at the corner store. I brought some gum and an oatmeal cake and two quarter waters, purple and blue. Yvette got some lime cookies and an apple juice.

I offered to pay; she said, "I got it." She had her own money. Thank God she paid for her things. I didn't have enough money, but I had to offer. Right outside the store, a fifty-dollar bill was balled up on the floor. The people in front of the store were rolling dice and arguing. I picked up the money so fast, without anybody noticing. Somebody started shooting in front of the store over a bag of weed. At the same time, a fight broke out in the store. Somebody had stolen a bottle of beer, and one of the Arab men working at the store got into a fistfight over the bottle of beer. We made it to the party safely. The line was moving fast. We made it inside in less than twenty minutes. I gave the fifty dollars to Mice to get us some drinks or whatever; he was the oldest and most knowledgeable. Mice made sure the crew was safe and together. It was about 3:00 a.m., and the party was just getting warmed up. Yvette and I got in for free. The people at the door assumed we had gone out for a cigarette. We walked inside for free. I had never seen anything like this—so many teenagers mingling. The group Full Force was playing "Ain't My Type of Hype." Everybody in the party had a cup of alcohol. Mice ordered everyone in the crew drinks. I had like five drinks, all different colors. The drinks kept on coming. I started dancing. With so many girls everywhere I turned, there was an available girl with no partner in sight. The girls were aggressive. I loved every minute of it. I forgot about Yvette. The alcohol got to me. This was the first time I had drunk so much. Yvette walked up to me in the middle of the dance floor. Yvette put her arms around my neck to slow dance, but the music was too fast. The DJ put the spotlight on us. Yvette was very shy. She walked off the dance floor laughing. I just stood there like a dummy, calling her to come back, but the spotlight wasn't her thing. I was under the influence of the weed and alcohol. I wanted more of the spotlight. I walked behind Yvette to pull her back on the dance floor. I felt someone grab my other hand. I looked back to see who was grabbing me. There were a group of girls. One of them was pointing at me, calling me toward the dance floor. The DJ put the spotlight on her.

I walked back in the middle of the dance floor, where the girls were; one of them approached me, and this girl whispered in my ear, with her tongue touching my ear, "What's your name?"

I whispered in her ear, "Who, me?"

She whispered back, "No, you, what's yours?" she said.

I said, "Will."

She said, "I'm Iesha." I wanted to put my tongue back in her ear, but I was afraid; plus, my body was excited. The DJ slowed things down a bit with some Zapp's "Computer Love." Naturally we danced together. She put her arms around me and got so close I pushed back. I didn't want her to feel my body changing; it was embarrassing. The more I pushed away, she hooked me tight like a boa constrictor and put her lips to my ear and said, "It's OK. I can feel you." We danced nearly five songs body to body. I looked across the room. Yvette was dancing with my friend Dice. I wanted to get away from Iesha. She was so beautiful; she had big, juicy lips and neat black-and-golden dreadlocks. I stepped outside to smoke a Newport. Mice and the crew were on the patio smoking a blunt.

Yvette stood near me and said. "How's your new girlfriend?" I just laughed. It wasn't funny, but it was the alcohol, and Iesha, that girl had the experience. Mice had a nice Cuban mommy;

he had just met Dice, who was after Yvette. The rest of our crew was just enjoying the atmosphere and mingling. Everybody was happy except Yvette, and I knew just how to make it up to her. The DJ was on point. The speakers on the patio were so loud. He was playing Mtume's "Juicy Fruit." I walked over to Yvette, and she pulled away from me and went back inside the club. Dice followed her after five minutes. I was planning to go spend time with her as soon as we finished the blunts. I asked one of my homegirls in our crew to talk to her. Tasha did and came back to tell me that Yvette wanted me to spend time with her. Tasha was a miracle worker; she had fixed things between us. Iesha held my nose open; we weren't dancing, more like having sex on the dance floor. She was way too close. When she felt me getting excited, she pressed against me harder. Iesha walked out onto the patio with her sister and three friends.

She walked right between my legs, and straight in my ear with her tongue, she asked me, "How old are you?"

I said, "Me?" She just looked at me. I said, "Seventeen," but truthfully I was going on fourteen.

I asked her, "How old are you?"

With her tongue in the frame of my ear, she said, "Nineteen," and walked back inside. She didn't like the smoke.

Mice said, "Boy, you better get on your job, fool. She is bad."

I said, "What about Yvette?"

Mice said, "Bro, if you blow this one…" The DJ kept the hits coming. He played Zhane's "Hey Mr. D.J." I was planning to go dance with Yvette, but Iesha's body was so curved and slim, like a Coca-Cola bottle—easily top ten at the party. I took a deep pull off my Newport. I was a virgin, but my crew always thought I was a vet and had had sex many times. I had no idea what I was doing. Around 3:45 a.m., 2 Live Crew preformed. I walked inside just in time for "Doo Doo Brown." I had never danced to this song before. I looked for Yvette. We made eye contact from across the room. There were many people still coming into the club. I stood near the DJ booth so Yvette could see me. She started walking slowly. I figured maybe she was mad at me or tired. Iesha was standing behind me with her girls; she didn't allow anyone to dance with her, which made me look like a superstar. The moment I made eye contact with Iesha, she jumped right on top of it; she grabbed my belt and held me close. She danced all between my legs to "Doo Doo Brown."

The entire club was looking at us, screaming, "Go, go, go!" The DJ put the spotlight on us; it felt like my birthday party. I got the hang of this dancing thing quick. Iesha was a good teacher. Things slowed down about 4:45. I gave Iesha some space and went over by the crew to chill. Mice was making out with his Cuban honey. Yvette and me talked for about ten minutes. I went to the bar to get another drink. When I returned, Yvette was dancing with Dude. Dice had found him some pretty big redbone. The DJ played slow jams and reggae the rest of the night. Mad Cobra's "Flex" was a big hit. Iesha still wasn't dancing with anybody. I walked up to her like a magnet. She jumped right back on me. At this point, my body was throbbing. The DJ knew just what to play. Mice decided to stay in Yonkers. The girl he was dancing with gave him the digits and left. I didn't care at this point. The little devil on my shoulder was right: my night was going well. Mice knew Yonkers and the Bronx well; he had grown up here before moving to Brooklyn. We had an invite to an after-party. I didn't want to leave, but the DJ started playing the same song he closed with: Chaka Demus's "Murder She Wrote." I got my last dance with Iesha. I didn't know the protocol, so I just told Iesha good night. Mice asked Iesha's sister to come to the after-party. They agreed. They drove. We called two taxis. Iesha and the girls waited until our taxi came and followed us. We made it to the after-party in ten minutes. The music was so loud, like it was 9:00 p.m. There were only two houses on the block. Mice knew the people. There was alcohol and food everywhere. Iesha made me a plate of food. I couldn't get her off me. She made me some chicken fried rice and corn bread with green beans. It wasn't easy to see; the entire house had red light bulbs in every room.

I was so hungry my plate was clean in five minutes; then Iesha said to me, "Have you said sex before?" In her face I could tell she knew that made me afraid. We moved the furniture out of the way and put the food in the kitchen. The DJ got right to it, starting things off with Color Me Badd. Iesha and I danced so close, like we were married with kids. Mice was with Iesha's sister. She was pretty. Yvette was dancing with Dice. Everybody found a corner. Iesha put her tongue down my throat. We went into a room; she took control of the entire situation. The rest is history. Life forces you to become grown overnight. There's so much pain in the black community that it is hard to notice the blessings of America; the next morning I walked Iesha and the girls to their car. They left at 8:00 a.m.; we exchanged information and kissed for like five minutes. Her sister and friend kept calling us lovebirds as they pulled off. She took my heart with her. Our taxi pulled up shortly after. We didn't stay to clean up. We made it to the subway at 9:00 a.m. and had a long ride back to Brooklyn. Everybody hopped the turnstile.

The clerk in the token booth said on the loudspeaker, "Pay your fare. I'm calling the police." I watched the clerk pick up the phone. The train was nowhere in sight. My heart was beating fast. We were the only black kids on the platform; the other nationalities were Hispanic and white. Segregation was a big part of American culture, like Confederate flags and monuments. The older generations of black people had been conditioned to accept this way of life; the younger generation is naive to the facts of life under the veil of ignorance.

AFTER-PARTY IESHA YVETTE

My generation is in a unique moment in time, where the veil of ignorance is being lifted. The American dream has always been upfront with the black community. Our problem is we can't face reality. Everybody sat down on the benches in the middle of the train platform. I never took my eyes off the clerk; an older white woman observed us kids illegally riding the train. The woman walked in my direction. She asked, "Why didn't you pay your fare?" My friends started laughing at the fact the white woman was questioning me without a care in the world. They didn't take it seriously. The woman looked right into my soul with her deep-blue, piercing eyes and reached into her purse and pulled out a twenty-dollar bill. My heart was racing so fast I thought she was reaching for a police badge. The white woman said to me with authority, "Take this money and go pay the fare of all of those kids." I did just what she told me to do before the woman closed her purse. I could smell the scent of peppermint coming from the bag, just like my grandmother. The closer I got to the token booth, the better I felt better. After I paid everybody's fare, the woman told me to keep the change, I was the only one to say thank you. I kept staring at the woman from head to toe. I didn't understand why she had helped us. I was confused and grateful. The lady took out from her bag some bread in a Ziploc plastic bag and fed the pigeons on the platform at first. I thought the woman was nuts, but I realized the white little old lady was just trying to fix the little things wrong with the world. I looked down the tracks and saw the train coming. A bright white light was moving very fast in our direction. After we boarded the train, we stood out from everyone else on board, who was dressed for church; in those days 90 percent of business in America were closed on Sunday to honor the concept of God in the Bible, the greatest story ever told. America was made up of different nationalities legally organized for segregation through the State Department. Most Americans believed diversity was a positive thing—unique individuals coming together from different ethnicities. This great experiment has turned into a tragedy. This melting pot of race, gender, and religious beliefs has given politician and mainstream media a reason to strip the rights away from the world. The truth is that in this great American experiment, the taxpayers are paying for was a very selfish racial adventure that created the civil rights movement and the original sin of America slavery, jim crow, sharecropping, and social injustice are all part of the never-ending story of global domination. The great experiment is like a medicated part—this global crime network the framers created is the makeup of slaves, refugees, and capitalists. The great experiment turned humans into a scientific product. Our country has been turned into a laboratory, and the people are the chemistry vials and testing subjects; the American dream is full of biological weapons in the form of food, medication, water, education, religion, prescription drugs, vaccines, and pesticides. The modern matrix is the American dream. The complex perception, also known as smoke screens, is a two-sided coin: on one side, there's opportunity and freedom; on the other side of the coin is a permanent underclass of people with no wealth or sovereignty. On our way back to Brooklyn, Yvette and I didn't say a word to each other; my mind was on Iesha and how could I explain my way out of being grounded by my mother. I started thinking about the 1979 movie *The Warriors* and how they made it back home in one piece. The consequences were worth it. The black community in America, strategically located near oil refineries and chemical power plants, suffers from chronic depression and biological mental disfigurement.

This unfortunate reality was complemented by religious and secular miseducation and wealth deficiencies. That was exactly why I didn't fear my mother's wrath. Our elders' prehistoric mind-set sheltered the youth from the reality of the American court system and political process yet exposed us to an enigma of Tartarus found in religious philosophy. Once the train stopped in Manhattan, a group of young black boys with a radio walked onto the train with a Chinese woman selling candy and toy. I brought a pack of Skittles and some AA batteries for my Walkman. The boys were trying to earn a living break-dancing. They played Sheila E.'s "The Glamorous Life." These boys were acrobats and could put the circus out of business. Entertainment is a necessary evil in the black community. After slavery our historical inability to obtain sovereignty led to a hamster wheel of skinning and grinning; we tried to entertain the dominant society for political favor and currency—a bag of money instead of recreating the institutions of financial independence for the next ten generations. As a result, my generation is wandering in the wilderness at the mercy of the Democrat and Republicans, entertaining the world for a bag of money. The industries of sports, music, television, and comedy have built a predator washing machine, drying the black community up in its own liabilities with no generational assets, just liquidated ignorance. I gave the boys one buck. Supporting black businesses using their God-given talents and abilities is very important. There are so many things in the black community that deserve deeper context. Ninety-nine point nine percent of the black existence on this planet is compartmentalized into four-hundred-plus year of slavery. Ages of recorded knowledge have been expunged from our memory. The obvious dysfunctions that are displayed in our everyday life leave a trail of evidence of a greater sinister plan, an apparatus of organized genocide. Racial epithets, fatherless homes, economic inequality, abortion, incarceration, housing injustice, and wealth gaps are peanuts and pale in comparison to the real problem; the lack of knowledge of self is what generates an artificial person. The invisible border patrol separating the black homes are policies and religious doctrines creating internal affairs compliance enforcement among the willfully ignorant of the idea of self-destruction based on a lack of information. Our willful blindness renders the current and next generation philosophical zombies, identical to our once-human selves but having no consciousness indistinguishable from mankind. This reality doesn't seem conceivably an entire race of people blinded by themselves; one could go to the extremities of their imagination and still couldn't perceive the wickedness of the diabolical condition the black community is in. A once-complex people are now operating off the physical substance called food—just the bare necessities. The system made the primary perpetrator of our demises our black selves, coached by the black church, the Democratic Party, and the State Department. No matter how atrocious America's history is, the unpleasant truth of the matter is that the framers of the Constitution, those fifty-five individuals appointed to draft the agreement of the Delaware maritime corporation, must be studied. I finally made it back to Brooklyn hungry and tired, ready for my punishment irony cord or belt. It didn't matter at this point. Respectfully, I had had enough of my parents' self-righteousness. I walked up the stairs and out of the subway onto the street, feeling like a new man with eight dollars in my pocket. I stopped at a local diner outside of the Kingston-Throop train station. I had only passed this place a hundred times; not once had I ever seen a black person inside, but, hungry and naïve, I walked right in and sat down. I was the only so-called Negro, not that the term *African* was any better—both Latin terms. All eyes were on me. Maybe I'd been naive my entire life—innocent, some might say. I had always seen white people as harmless and nonthreatening. My generation had never felt the real anxiety or racism the previous generations had dealt with. I was born in New York City, or the North, to be correct. It's modern-day slavery. The only young person in the joint was a young white girl waiting tables. She had to be at least sixteen, with working papers. She came to my table and poured me a glass of OJ. I didn't know what to order, but everything looked great. I ordered bacon and eggs with a side of hash browns and two waffles. All of that came to six dollars—extremely impressive. I waited for my food, thinking about the night before and my mother's reaction. All kinds of excuses came to my mind. The best one was that I had fallen asleep watching a movie at my friend's house. My food came to the table nice and hot. I was starving metaphorically; my eyes were bigger than my belly. I poured half of the table condiments onto my plate: salt and pepper; ketchup. My pancakes were swimming in syrup. My face looked like an easel painted with sauce. The waitress came over to check on me. She asked, "How's the food?" I nodded yes. As she refilled my cup with orange juice, she poured it very slowly, lifting the container high and lowering it down. I stopped to look around. I forgot other people were in the diner. All eyes were on me. Every white family was looking in my direction, smiling like they were in a photo shoot. One couple passed by my table and dropped twenty dollars on near my plate and kept walking. Another older white women came up to my table and squeezed my cheeks and placed ten dollars on the table. I was confused. The waitress brought out more food. She removed my plate and placed another round of food. I wasn't worried about the cost, but I called the waitress over to my table to ask for the check. She told me somebody had paid already with a fifty-dollar bill and brought me the change. No kidding, I was freaked out, but I kept on eating. The jukebox was playing. Someone picked the song "Then He Kissed Me," by the Crystals. It felt like it brought life to the diner; the music was nice. The next song that played was the Tokens' "The Lion Sleeps Tonight," then Bobby Darin's "Dream Lover." This diner was classy. Everyone that left said bye after they finished dancing. I was well fed with sixty bucks in my pocket. White people were all right with me. The Bee Gees' "More than a Woman" was the last song to play. The waitress asked me what school I attended and how old I was. She was cute and nosy. I told her PS 183 off Riverdale Avenue, District 23, and I was fourteen years old. She laughed and said, "That was my old school. Stop clowning. If you're fourteen years old, you're too old to go there." She said, "No, really, what school do you go to?"

I told her, "Boys and Girls High School."

She said to me, "I never saw you there before." The truth of the matter is that we were between homes. My mother and father had just split. I said thank you, collected my money, and left the diner. My mother had just become a single mom. After she signed up for public assistance, my father wasn't allowed to live with us, according to the State Department. After my mother signed up for Section 8 housing control, the state required my father to leave the premises, but he'd always come back every night after eight o'clock until the state learned about this from the social worker who came to our house every month to check that no men were in the home. The social worker recommended a group of private investigators from the state welfare department set up a surveillance team around the house to spy on us to make sure no men were in the home. I started walking home slowly and thinking I heard a female voice telling me to wait just a minute. It was the waitress from the diner. I had paid for my food, what could she want? I stopped and waited for her to catch up. She told me she had just gotten off work. She said her name was Diana. She said normally rode the bus this way but wanted to walk today because the weather was very nice.

I asked her, "Where are you from?" She told me Brooklyn, but her mother was Colombian, and her father was Russian and lived in Brighton Beach near Coney Island. Her mother had lived in Crown Heights for ten years.

She put her headphone on my ears and said, "Listen to this." She didn't ask me if it was OK. She had a very nice Walkman with a radio. I pressed play. The song she was listening to was number one on the pop charts, Mariah Carey's "Dreamlover." I could see through the glass cover of the Walkman that the tape was a mix from Doo Wop, *Cool Out '93*, a hip-hop mixtape. She was jamming. Incredible—she looked just like Mariah, with a giant butt like a black girl. Suddenly I felt she understood the struggle at least a little—the music truly bridged the gap. Diana had very long, curly deep-black hair and honey-brown eyes with light-brown skin. We came to my block. I handed her back her Walkman. She invited me to a friend's birthday party at the Empire skating rink the next week. I told Diana that would be cool. She told me to hold her Walkman and bring it with me the next week; then she kissed me on the cheek. I watched her walk away, feeling bad I was looking at a white girl. What was more disturbing, she had the biggest round butt in Brooklyn. I loved America and didn't have time to be afraid. I walked up to my door. It was almost 10:30 a.m. The front door was open. My older sister had just got back in the house; she had stayed out all night. Keisha knew my mother wasn't coming home until later that afternoon.

My older sister thought I had gotten up early that morning and gone outside. Unbeknownst to me, I had had nothing to worry about. Nobody knew I was gone except Danielle, and I had paid her off with twenty dollars I'd gotten from the diner. My older sister brought Danielle and me some McDonald's and candy. She made us promise not to tell. We promised. The three of us had a good understanding of things. My mother was a very busy woman between the Democratic Party and the church. My dad was very different; he was an old-school Republican party-of-Lincoln kind of guy. With my father out of the home, we just followed my mother's political viewpoints. All my friends had the same issues. Their fathers were gone through the same program of the Democratic Party. For 80 percent of the black community in New York City, suddenly one day all the fathers disappeared overnight—systemic social engineering organized by our State Department. This centralized, planned attack was a deliberate assault on the black family from the dominant society, whoever that might be. This was an attempt to manage social regulations and future development to manipulate the behavior of each generation: cognitive behavior therapy, the great American experiment. Side effects of a black male with no father in the home: anxiety, depression, panic attacks, eating disorders, anger, phobias, crime, suicide—with a toxic mother to top it off.

THE DINER AND DIANA WALKMAN

With the tragedy of the black Christian woman divorcing the black man and marrying the State Department, the system moved into control of our generation, slavery all over again, and the children had no way to fight with the fathers gone. The control system over the black community goes as such: the Jewish community controls the Democratic Party, which controls the black woman, who controls the children and the black church. "The great American experiment": public factory schools; religious recycling; church; media; misleading histograms; historical negationism; historical revisionism; historical distortion; alteration of the black community; hellfire; wealth bewilderment; Tartarus; deep mental phobias; mental torment of the abyss dungeon. With the fathers out of the picture, it was smooth sailing for the Democratic Party; the party had a covenant with black Christian women to maintain the matrix, the artificial mental enforcement orientation program. The idea is to ensure an inevitable, unavoidable imprisonment state of mind using black mothers to create the negative black-broken-home narrative so the state will look like it's only trying to help. The document is the new slavery; it handcuffs the language and method of computing the system's communication to the human brain: the United States versus the United States of America; the State of New York versus New York State; parent versus guardian; marriage license versus civil union; driving versus traveling; sovereignty versus liberty. The language of casting spells is (s)words: *mind your business*; *pay attention*; *pay them no mind*; *pay my respects*; *money grows on trees*; *cash flow*; *river bank of money*; *currency*. The television played a huge role in painting roses on our glasses. Shows like *Good Times*, *The Jeffersons*, *Martin*, *Fresh Prince*, *Sanford and Son*, *The Cosby Show*, and *Family Matters* gave the black community a glimpse of hope, the good life, so the TV tells you your vision. I walked around the house thinking and reflecting on the party in Yonkers. I was wondering what Iesha was doing and if she was thinking about me. I didn't regret a moment. My soul felt free for the first time to experience America. The only reason my generation is ignorant of the workings of society is our elders' leadership. They're not leading us to the architect of creation; the real objective is to redirect our attention using a familiar face we call our parents to detour each generation so we don't carry the torch of our ancestors' achievements. Our ancestors left us a war chest of illumination, enlightenment, and intellectual sovereignty. I always wondered how our elders had gone astray to abort the mission of meaningful free. I believe under the influence of politics, polytheism, and theocracy, which seems wholesome and to have holistic benefits, 95 percent of Christian black women would prefer to hand their children a Bible instead of the Constitution. Black fathers prefer to hand their boys boxing gloves, basketballs, and footballs instead of a constitutional law dictionary—real stepping stones, substantive firm pillars, versus hope and faith, which I call the veil of ignorance. Our black parents' ideology of religious regiments destroys all basic common sense and consciousness of old Negro spiritual superstition. Please don't get me wrong. I respect individuals' personal belief systems. I feel like it's radical indoctrination. I lay on my bed listening to Diana's Doo Wop mixtape, *Cool Out '93*, thinking about next week's birthday party at the Empire skating rink. What I thought about the most were my feelings for Diana, which had started already. I think Yvette's and my relationship was done. Maybe I was just young, but Iesha was worth spending the time with. I worried about calling her, but my mother would never let me have a girlfriend. To me, age was just a number. Most of the thing I experienced had been by trial and error. To me, curiosity didn't kill the cat; it trained the cat. If I had to sum up my childhood in one-word feelings, it was all about the emotional roller coaster. Feelings alternate so fast between sad, happy, horny, disappointed, desperate, embarrassed, bored, and confused. Our mood swings cause disorders and depression. The black community's bipolar syndromes are made worse by religion and miseducation. Black women are so powerfully, naturally mysterious; their enigmatic power is expressed through perfume, lingerie, Nubian hair, and sex appeal. The black woman is much more than that, but the radiance emanating from her mind is holy—something to do with her being God. The wisdom of Eve eating the fruit is a lot deeper than people think. The reason the devil went after Naive, or Eve, is that she was smarter than Adam and had the power to bring him and the family down—kind of like the black woman. Both of them talk with snakes, and their children pay the price. When growing up in a Christian home, the story that is heard makes no sense from Genesis to Revelation. I believe the real story is that the woman had influence over the man, and the devil knew she could get him to disobey God, but the man wouldn't be able to influence her to lose her home. I go based on the facts of life, especially the black woman's order of priorities: Jesus, shelter, children, clothing, food, money, than a man, The black man's order of priorities is sex, car, sports, gold, then children. Religion is in every aspect of black people's lives; it's something we picked up in slavery. Religion permeates every strand of the institution of the human being, from marriage to our livelihood, child-rearing, education, and even thinking. Religion is like an internet browser. The only way to access anything is to go through the web of religion, surrendering full control over one's mind, never allowing one to have an independent mental operating system based solely on consciousness and science. I never talked with my family about, you know, the birds and the bees. I call this a specialized curriculum. In the black community, it seems forbidden to speak about ordinary things citizens are concerned about. The only conversation we had was centered around ecclesiastical matters; other normal topics like finances, farming, ancestry, stocks, law, the Constitution, civil service, and things associated with freedom were deemed unworthy and not a part of the doctrine of ecclesiastical matters. This doctrine is a covenant of creed signed by the slave masters and the slaves postslavery. If anything, they should free the slave. A promise was made to only allow the slave master to educate the slave children to ensure there was no hate being thought. The doctrine of ecclesiastical matters is like a ham sandwich: bread, meat, and mayo. The only things our parents were allowed to teach us in the black community were the Bible, European history, and respect for the law. The entire black community should be on CBT (cognitive behavioral therapy) instead of police brutality, prescription medicines, and welfare. I mean welfare from the dominant society through housing, community college, social programs, and employment in exchange for our vote; these are just temporary handouts, parting gifts. Like Dr. Martin Luther King Jr. said, this doesn't solve the real problem. I sure did miss my dad. Once we came back from the bookstore, which was closed, my mother broke the news to my father about the State Department wanting him out of the home for my mother's benefits to continue.

The state had sent a special group called the EVR (Eligibility Verification Review) to watch the house and seen my dad coming in and out of the home. One of the social workers had checked our home and counted the toothbrushes; she had assumed the extra one was for Dad and set up a face-to-face hearing to investigate fraud. The EVR unit had set up a board meeting that gave my mother one last chance to tell Dad to get lost. They had shown her the pictures they had taken and the witness's statements, which would have been enough to convict Mom of fraud and cheating on the state with another man. As much as I missed my dad, all I could think about was Iesha and the unusual thunderstorm that had blown in and knocked out all the power in the neighborhood. I heard a bolt of loud, booming lightning hit a transfer. My grandmother had told us thunderstorms were fights between God and the devil. I used to pee in the bed after dreaming of hellfire and all the biblical stories associated with the rapture. Thunderstorms always made those stories resurface. I didn't get much sleep that night, and the batteries in Diana's Walkman were dying. The next morning my mother came home around 9:00 a.m. She brought coffee and doughnuts. Her favorite coffee was Sanka. I wasn't enrolled in school yet because we were on Section 8 temporary housing, so my mother came home to tell my sister the good news she had gotten from the welfare department: they had found us a home in Jamaica, Queens, and we had to leave immediately. My heart dropped. I had so many friends in Brooklyn. The house would be ready in three weeks, but our landlord wanted us out by the end of the week. He had a couple who was paying cash. The welfare department took too long to pay our landlord. The landlord had given my older sister a final notice to give to my mother. He was going to lock the door at the end of the week. I was listening to my mother's conversation, but I couldn't ascertain much. I was pissed off. Suddenly I heard the door slam. I walked in the front room. My mother left. I asked my sister, "What did Mom say?"

She just told me, "Mom had to leave. A friend of hers died, so she had to run out." I just walked out of the house and slammed the door. My sister yelled down the hallway, "Get back here. I'm telling Mommy." I knew where to find my friends, on the corner or in the park. We were supposed to pack and get ready to leave before the landlord locked the door. I had my Walkman and a pack of batteries I had bought on the subway from a Chinese woman. I was only going to chill with my friends for an hour or so, just to clear my head. My life was being shaped by my parents' trial and era. By the time I became an adult, I would have spent my whole life trying to unravel their veil of ignorance, knitted and woven into my generation to arrest our development. Sacrifice is better than obedience. It just seems from the time your birth certificate is created, the objective is to have your guardian or parents perform a ceremony of Tartarus, a mental christening. The ceremony is a voluntary cognitive prison. Everything about church and school, social society, dominates our human experience and individuality in a cultlike way, blocking consciousness and responsiveness. The system is controlling youth perception and awareness, stifling their brains by artificially creating genetically modified altered beings or mannequins using engineering techniques. I caught up to my friends hanging out at the game room. The arcade was huge. I got five dollars' worth of quarters. One quarter went a long way with me. Finally, I could clear my mind. Subconsciously, Iesha was still walking around in my head—just growing pains. I didn't tell my friends we had to move. I still couldn't believe it and considered running away. My brain felt like it was overheating. I spent the whole day playing games. I didn't realize the time, but the sun was going down. My favorite games were *NBA Jam* and *Pac-Man*. After the arcade my friends went to the park to see a pit bull fight a boxer for money. I had to get home. My mother was strict. Plus I knew Keisha would exaggerate when I left the house and slammed the door. When I got to the house, the lights were off, and the window I left open was locked, and my key was inside the house. I sat on the porch for about two hours, hungry and frustrated, and my batteries died in the Walkman. I rolled up a little joint and smoked as I walked toward the park, but the weed making me even more hungry, so I walked the other way, toward the diner and straight into the bathroom to pee. I was so high I forgot Diana was working at the diner.

The waitress already knew what I wanted; she said out loud as I ran toward the restroom, "The usual?"

I said, "Yes, with a Coke." Diana wasn't there, but the waitress called to tell her I was eating. Just before I finished my food, Diana walked in and went straight into the kitchen. After about five minutes, Diana came and sat at my table. She said she had come to drop off some keys from the job that she had taken home by mistake. After I ate we walked back toward the house. I had so many questions for her, like where did she get that mixtape and did she like basketball. She said yes to everything. I took a good look at her for the first time. She was beautiful.

Her eyes were deep green, and her hair was very curly, and she had natural pink lips. We walked to my house because I was late, but the light to my apartment was still off. My friends Mice and Dice was sitting on my porch smoking a blunt. My mother hated me hanging out with them. The front door to my apartment was locked. This was a first. Mice was the leader of our crew. He told me we had to go to a mandatory Crip meeting and to tell Diana to go home. I told her I would talk to her later. She started to walk away, looking back every ten steps. Just before me and the crew turned the corner to go to the park, Diana ran back toward us. She begged me to walk her halfway home. She said she was afraid. I looked at Mice. He told me to make it quick. We walked back toward my apartment.

The landlord noticed me and asked, "Where is your mother?" I told him I wasn't sure. He told me if he didn't get his rent by tomorrow night, he would throw our things on the street. I was so embarrassed that Diana had heard all of that. On the way toward her house, I sparked up the blunt and convinced Diana to take two pulls off the blunt. We had so many things in common. She was a Knicks fan and loved Tupac. Before I noticed we were in front of her house, she started crying. I thought it was the weed, but she wouldn't tell me what was wrong. She just kept asking me to spend the night. I told her my crew needed me—it was important.

Then she kissed me slow and long and said, "Wait here one second."

I was thinking maybe she was locked out, too, but her mother came to the door and said, "Will you come inside just for a moment? I heard about you. Let me have a look at you."

I was thinking only five minutes—Mice was going to kill me. I walked inside their home; it was very nice. Diana's mother was even more beautiful than she was; in some ways, she looked like a teenager. She was a beautiful Spanish woman with hair down to her butt, with a bigger butt than Diana. I wasn't looking; It's just impossible not to notice. She made me some hot chocolate and a plate of food. I couldn't say no. She made some curry chicken peas and rice, with some Kool-Aid. I didn't notice right away. Diana's mother had dreadlocks; she was a registered nurse and worked overnight, twelve to twelve, three nights a week. Diana mom was a huge Bob Marley fan; she had four different pictures of him with quotes in the living room on her wall. She left me and Diana in the room and got dressed for work.

I told Diana, "The guys are waiting on me."

Her mother came out of the room wearing scrubs with a T-shirt, and her butt was moving everywhere. Somehow she knew I noticed it because I was looking everywhere except at her. She kept asking me, "Are you all right?" I felt like the room was an oven. Diana went into her room and changed into a white silk nightgown, and her butt was everywhere. It was so hard for me to stand up. I just sat there with both of my arms covering my lap. Diana's mother played some reggae, and they invited me to dance. I wanted to, but if I stood up, they would notice I was excited. They just danced together so close that I almost melted. Diana's mother said her boyfriend was coming to take her to work and would drop me off at my house. Her mother's boyfriend was Jamaican, Mr. Winston. He knocked on the door like a cop. He worked security part time and sold weed on the side. We all walked outside to get in the car. Diana's mom told me to call her "Mommy." It was her childhood nickname. She didn't like me saying "Ms. Hernandez"; she said it made her feel old. Winston had a hype sound system. I and Diana were holding hands in the backseat; Mommy turned the music down like a block away from my house, and Winston started slowing down. I noticed Diana's face looking at the police cars on my block. My heart was pumping. Yellow tape blocked off any entry into my block. The police stopped us from getting any closer. As he approached the vehicle on the side of the drive, Winston rolled the window down. The officer asked if we lived here. Mommy sad yes. The officer said to park and walk inside. There were two ambulances on the block. The closer I got to my house, I saw people were crying.

Yvette ran toward me and hugged me tight. She said, "They killed Mice and Dice." I dropped to my knees in disbelief.

The rest of the crew came over to me and said, "Two eleven—let's go ride." They knew who had done it.

I told Diana, "Sorry, my crew needs me." They had a stolen car a few blocks away.

Yvette said, "Let's go there behind the projects, near the circle."

Diana hugged me tight with tears in her eyes. She kissed me in front of her mother. She said, "Please don't." She whispered in my ear. She was crying because earlier she had dreamed a boy died, but she couldn't see his face.

The crew said, "Let's go now."

Diana said, "Please don't. The boy was you." She said he had died in water that was blue like paint, and she couldn't save him because she was afraid to see his face. I backed up from Diana and ran toward Winston's car and sat near the front tire crying in my lap. Diana came and cried with me. We all got in the car and headed back toward the house. Mommy told Winston to stop at the store to get some ginger; she wanted to make me some tea. She wanted to take the night off. Diana told her it was OK; she'd take care of me.

Mommy said, "Are you sure?"

Diana said, "Yes."

Winston's car phone rang while he was in the store. Mommy answered it, thinking it was Winston calling from the store phone to ask her what else she needed. All I heard was "Who is this?" then "Really? For how long?" and "What's your name?" It was Winston's wife. Mommy didn't know about her or Winston's eight kids. Mommy hung up the phone and didn't say a word until we got home. She made me some tea and went to work like nothing had ever happened. She called the house twenty minutes later to check on me and Diana. She said she would be off tomorrow; she'd worked for her three days, and we'd have a meeting tomorrow. After Diana hung up the phone, she massaged my legs and feet with coconut oil and my back. I had so many things on my mind. Diana poured more hot water into my cup and lit my blunt. She said it was OK to smoke in the house for tonight. Diana opened up the windows in the house, and the cold air brought in the reality of my friend's death. We had just been at a party together laughing and talking. This felt like a nightmare. All that I could think about was the crew and revenge. Diana went in the room and changed back into her white nightgown. I had no idea where my mother and sisters where. Diana played some soft reggae music from Judy Mowatt,

"Mellow Mood." She kissed me so slowly we could taste each other's tears. We kissed all night long. I laid my face in her lap. I could smell her sweet cinnamon skin through her gown while she twisted my hair. Diana took out the pullout bed from the sofa and made it nice for me. Then she lit two candles. The music got louder, or the weed kicked in. She removed her clothes, but I couldn't see anything. She was wearing a shiny necklace. This was all I could see. Her eyes were glowing green, and the ball around her neck lit up in bright letters: "Pangaea." I tried to stand up. My vision was blurry, and the room was spinning, but it felt good. She kept laughing. The room was dark, and the music was loud. I kept trying to grab her, but she was too fast. All I could see were her glowing green eyes. I closed my eyes and relaxed. When I opened my eyes, she was on top of me. Her hair smelled like insects. She moved on top of me. It felt like heaven, but her nails were so deep into my back she was ripping my skin, but it didn't hurt. I woke up looking around. Diana was in her room sleeping in her white gown. I was dreaming. I wondered if the weed mixed with the ginger had made me dream that amazing fantasy. Just to make sure, I checked to see if Diana was wearing a neckless. It had just been a dream. Mommy came home early and made breakfast. We ate in the kitchen like a family. Mommy told Diana that Winston was married, and she didn't want to speak to him. The phone rang for hours once she came home. Mommy asked me to stay one more night to make sure things were OK. Diana had work that afternoon from two until six. I walked her to work. On our way to her job, we walked through my block. The landlord had put all of our things out in the front yard. I didn't have much, just some clothes and shoes;

next to my things there was a black box that had written on the top "Pangaea." I felt like it had a familiar ring to it.

Yvette walked up behind me and said, "What happened to you? Mice and Dice were your friends, and who is this white bitch? So it's like that. First Iesha, now Snow White. You watch your back, traitor." She walked away.

Diana didn't say much. She gave me her key and said, "Go home." I walked home back to her house, thinking that what Yvette had said hurt like hell, but what if Diana hadn't told me to walk her home? And her dream had my mind playing tricks on me. I got to the house with a heavy heart and an overheated brain. My crew had disowned me, or was Yvette right? I put my things in Diana's room. Mommy was in her room, probably sleeping from working overnight. So many things were happening at once. My dad would have been a big help right now. Somehow God was keeping me protected. The phone kept ringing nonstop all afternoon. I still managed to doze off to sleep until the doorbell rang, and someone was knocking on the door like the fire department. The phone just kept ringing; on the caller ID, Winston's name was popping up. It had just started to rain and was going to rain the rest of the week. He had picked the worst time to mess up. The knocking just continued. Finally Winston started knocking on the window on the side of the house, but the neighbor's dogs kept barking. Mommy came out of the room in a green T-shirt and green panties like thongs. I kept my eyes close like I was asleep and didn't hear anything. She was peeking through the peephole; then she unplugged all the phones in the house. Winston kept knocking. Mommy woke me up and told me to go sleep in her bed. I just did it, no questions asked. She waited until the knocking stopped and called a cab and went to pick up Diana. I was worried that Winston would see her or come in the house while they were gone. The rain picked up, and the sky darkened fast; then there was a bang on the window. Winston had come back. I could see his eyes through the blinds of the window, but the rain was so heavy he could barely see anything. After the one knock, that was it. Maybe the rain had gotten to him. The raindrops on the window seal put me to sleep; finally I heard the door close and Diana's voice. They had brought food back for me, and while I ate they covered the windows in Mommy's room with black garbage bags. The rain just kept falling from the sky; heaven was overflowing. Diana and Mommy took showers at the same time in different bathrooms. As weird as things were, I felt safe. Diana said, "We're gonna sleep in the room with Mommy and watch movies." They had ice cream and snacks. Diana was wearing a T-shirt and panties. She lit some sage and candles. She walked the sage all through the house. Mommy came out of the bathroom in a T-shirt and panties (black thong). She turned on reggae music and lit a blunt. Me and Mommy smoked while Diana picked out a movie. She chose *House Party*. Diana fixed the snacks in the kitchen, and Mommy was talking to her sister in Colombia on the phone in Spanish. Mommy and Diana spoke in Spanish in the house and started teaching me. It was easy. I lay in the bed playing *Tetris* on Diana's Game Boy, vibing to the reggae music, and enjoying the ganja. Diana played the movie, and we ate the snacks and laughed. After the movie, Diana made me a bed on the floor with like five blankets and three pillows. Me and Mommy smoked like three blunts. I took a shower. Diana gave me a towel and toothbrush. She took my clothes and washed them. They turned the movie off. I could hear the reggae music in the bathroom. From the corner of my eye, in the mirror I saw that my back had markings carved like with a knife. I panicked and dropped the soap and hit the light switch. I could hear the girls laughing. The music kept telling me to relax. The voice and lyrics were righteous. I opened the door. All the lights were off in the house. I wasn't afraid. The music was so powerful and righteous, with a soulful message. I walked into the living room. There were candles lit all around the house. Diana and Mommy were dancing with no clothes on, but I couldn't see their bodies. My vision was blurry. The more I relaxed, the closer they got. I lit the blunt in the ashtray and danced all over the house with both of them, at times separately. They knew what I wanted, so they dance with me in the middle. I felt and smelled every part of their bodies. I just couldn't touch them with my hands. It was so real. I was yelling. Diana woke me up. It had been a dream. Mommy asked me if I had had a nightmare. I looked around the room, and their faces were sleeping. I didn't know whether to like what was happening to me or stop smoking weed. They wanted to know what was in my dream. The rain was so heavy, and the thunder so loud. Diana made me get in the bed with them. Diana was in the middle. No more weed for me—I was under too much stress. Then again, that weed ain't bad.

DIANA, MOMMY WINSTON: WEED OR DREAM?

Morning with Diana and Mommy was beautiful. It started with burning sage and incense. Some Beres Hammond and

Buju Banton, "Pull It Up," played at the table for breakfast every morning. Like a family, we played board games almost every night. Hungry Hungry Hippos and Trouble were my favorites. Diana was the best at checkers. Mommy loved chess—that game was too complicated for me. The girls knew how to keep me in the house: good food, music, panties, and bras. There was nothing outside but crime, police, and the unknown—gangs and whatnot. The next morning, Mommy went grocery shopping and to her LA Fitness class, Diana and I went to Coney Island to visit her father. He had a new girlfriend. They took us to the Astroland amusement park. Her dad couldn't keep his hands off his new girlfriend; they were busy dating like kids, kissing every minute. Me and Diana had to watch them. Diana's father was a Russian who liked Run-DMC and old-school hip-hop like Big Daddy Kane and Slick Rick. Her father was a DJ. His girlfriend was a thick black woman; she was a hairstylist. It was kind of weird walking with Diana's father, a Russian man with two gold hoop earrings and a rope chain with a hand full of rings. Everybody called him Skip, and he was one of the best in New York City. Now I knew where Diana had gotten her mixtape from. On the weekend Skip hosted a radio show—this man had every record ever made. Skip was blacker than most black people I knew. His girlfriend was a little on the chubby side, her backside a bubble donkey. We went back to his house and ate pizza and watched *Ninja Turtles*. Skip and Antoinette, his girlfriend, had a wedding do and went to set the place us. Antoinette was a part-time wedding planner. After the movie, Diana and I walked to the store. She brought a Hostess apple pie and a pack of candles. The sun was setting. We took some blankets and found a nice spot under the boardwalk. I'd forgotten my birthday was yesterday. Diana had remembered and put two candles in the pies and sang me "Happy Birthday." it was the most beautiful sky, and the sound of the ocean was magnificent. We made it back home just in time. Mommy took a taxi from Western Beef to the house. Diana and me helped her bring the bags into the house. The taxi driver was from Pakistan and wanted to get Mommy's number. She paid him and took his card, just in case. The death of my friends Mice and Dice was still on my mind. One of the downsides of being on Section 8 housing was that the state always put the single-parent black women in drug-infested communities—the affordable housing trap. We watched a movie called *The Neverending Story*. This was Diana's all-time favorite. This was not just a kid's movie; there were so many subliminal messages. That movie resonated with my soul because I felt like I was reading my own story sometimes. We played Monopoly, the three of us. Diana handled the money, and Mommy handled the property—just like women, controlling everything. The way we played in the ghetto, the games were no fun unless everyone was cheating. Diana and Mommy played by the rules, which made the game more complicated. We played some old-school reggae and soca music. The girls loved music like a fish loves water. We cleaned up the house, and everybody took a shower and got ready for bed. I finished first and lay on the bed Diana had made for me on the floor. I smoked half of the blunt left over from yesterday and took two shots of Jack Daniel's for my birthday. The girls came into the room with no clothes on. This time I could see their bodies. They asked me to be completely honest. They wanted to know if this was what I desired, a beautiful mother and daughter making love to me at the same time I said yes. Mommy brought the black box with "Pangaea" written on it and opened the box; a hologram-like image appeared. I saw my life through the hologram image—every minute of my life. The wicked things I'd done, all my deeds, were recorded. Diana brought out a scale and placed it near the black box; both of them were wearing a necklace with a ball attached to it. The ball around Diana's neck read "Pangaea," and the ball around mommy's neck read "Saturn." Diana pointed out all my good deeds. Mommy pointed out all of the negative deeds. They made love to me, both of them, all over the house—my every pleasure. Every inclination of my heart was between their legs and between mine. Everything I wanted out of life I felt when they kissed me and had intercourse with me for hours. On both of their foreheads were circles, like yin and yang; the colors was blue and red and moving in a circular motion. Once we finished intercourse, the blue part of the circle on Mommy's forehead was bright; the blue part of the circle on Diana's forehead was bright red. Mommy lit candles all around us in a circle. Diana lit sage and placed them in a triangle inside the circle. They spoke to each other in the frequency sounds of Saturn and Pangaea, the sound 7.83.

Diana said, "They're following you. They're all around you. Your paradigm is an artificial matrix. The fire is in the middle. You must balance it." Diana told me to close my eyes. I felt her snatch my heart right out of my chest; it didn't hurt. I tried to open my eyes, but I wasn't able to.

Then Mommy took a feather from her hair; she said, "Close your mouth." I tried to speak, but I wasn't able to. Mommy placed the feather on the scales and said to me, "Cover your ears." I wasn't able to hear.

Then Diana said, "Use your pineal gland to see."

Mommy said, "Use your chakra to hear."

Than Diana said, "Use your stomach to speak." I was able to see, hear, and speak again, this time on the frequency of Saturn and Pangaea. Diana placed my heart on the scales, and my life flashed before my eye. I wasn't able to lie or turn away from my deeds. I heard the good and the bad loud and clear. Two females judged me. Diana said, "I am the sun."

Mommy said, "I am the moon, and you came from the stars after the great war." My bad deeds outweighed my good deeds. Then Mommy said, "In the judgment of Saturn, you shall not be born. Do you accept the verdict? As I began to answer, a woman with a lioness head appeared standing near a large glass tanklike casket. Mommy said, "You're going to go with her to the Sheol."

Diana said, "I object, Your Honor. There's more on the hologram." I saw my life as a polar bear and hyena and penguin. Diana said, "Is this part of his life as well?" The scale balanced, and the woman with the casket disappeared into the darkness.

They asked me at the same time, "Do you have any questions for us?"

I said, "Yes, just who are you?"

They both said, "We're the western oracle that sits at the corona of the firmament, the magnetic field of the belts around Pangaea." Diana and Mommy stood and walked backward into the darkness. They became one, like yin and yang. I woke up in my bedroom in my body. I looked under my bed to see if the black box was still there. It was gone, and the time was 8:04 p.m.

I got up out of the bed and walked into my parents' room. The house was empty. My sister was gone. Then the phone rang in the kitchen.

My mother said, "Where have you been?"

I said, "I'm not sure."

She said, "The landlord locked the doors. How did you get into the house?" I had no idea. My mother said, "The first thing in the morning, get on the train and go to your Aunt Karen's house. Your sisters are there." I hung up the phone and ran downstairs. The yellow tape was still outside.

I asked one of the crackheads walking by what had happened. "Why is there yellow tape all around the block?"

He said, "Where you been? Mice and Dice was killed yesterday." I ran to Diana's house. My memories were coming back to me the closer I got to her house. I got to the house and knocked on the doors. I could see a TV light in the window. The light outside the first porch turned on. I could hear the locks on the door turn; then the door opened. A man came to the door looking confused. I asked him where Diana and her mother were.

The man said, "I'm sorry. You have the wrong home." I pushed past the man and ran inside the house. His wife and children looked surprised. The man ran behind me, shouting, "Leave my home!" The woman grabbed the telephone to call the cops.

I dropped to my knees crying my soul out. "Diana, Mommy, please, God, no, not again."

The man took the phone from his wife and said, "Are you all right, mister? Who are you looking for? We've lived here at this house for ten years." I pulled myself together and apologized.

The man asked if I needed to call someone and where my parents were. Was I hungry? Did I need any money? With tears in my eyes, I said no and walked outside. The family walked behind me, looking puzzled. I walked back toward my house. There were nothing inside but memories. My mother wanted us to stay with my Aunt Karen until our house in Jamaica, Queens, was ready. I wanted to walk the block one last time and say goodbye to some choice people, but my better judgment said no way. See, we all think the streets love us and campaign on our behalf. It's just the opposite. The streets are a graveyard with a stomach. It's always hungry for fast food: young, inexperienced snacks. I didn't know what was going on in this world. All I knew was nothing worked the way we'd been brought up to believe and we had less time than we'd been told. To me, there's no such a thing as a childhood in this world. Ignorance is no excuse. The system starts the indoctrination in the womb; then the Cartoon Network takes over the church, school, the workplace. Then just follow the yellow brick road. The next morning I left for the Bronx early. At 6:00 a.m., I stopped at the diner I thought Diana worked at and got a bagel with cream cheese and a glass of orange juice. I asked the waitress at the diner what happened to Diana. She told me she'd never heard of her. I took the subway up to the Bronx the ride brought back memories of Yonkers. I had memorized Iesha's phone number. She lived off Fox Street near Hunts Point, about a ten-minute drive from my aunt's place. My Aunt Karen lived in the heart of the ghetto, but the crime rate was very low because the community was made up of nosy old women looking out the window and older men sitting outside playing dominoes; they kept a close eye on things. The

Bronx, out of all the five boroughs, felt like a village—just what my generation needed. The streets were a project every organization and institution was working on, from law enforcement to politicians, clergy, universities, special interest groups, activists, corporate America, and nonprofits. Go figure that one nonprofit, the children, were in the middle of it all. I had no idea what to tell my mother and Aunt Karen. I wasn't sure where I'd been. I missed Diana and Mommy. There had to be an explanation. What if I had gone to the wrong house? OK, but how did I explain the diner? They said they'd never heard of Diana. I had a hard time letting go and accepting life. The cards I was dealt always seemed like a bad hand, but I had learned how to play the hand. That's what had made me think and work with very little—that had to count for something. I made it to my aunt's house. She was sitting by the window. She probably saw me first. My Aunt Karen had the best seat on the block. She could see everything going on in the community from her window. Before I could say hi and go inside the house, my aunt sent me to the store to get a pack of cigarettes.

She handed me the money out the window and said, "Take fifty cents and bring my change back." My aunt smoked Virginia Slims, and all the stores in the community knew her, so I was able to buy the cigarettes with no problem. My aunt gave me the phone to speak with my mother when I came back from the store. My mother ordered me to stay in the house and not to watch television. My Aunt Karen didn't agree. She felt a boy belonged outside, so I was able to go outside, but I had to be in the house before the street lights came on. To me, my punishment was like being in a concentration camp. The first thing I did was go to the barbershop. Back then, men were more comfortable in the barbershop than in church; we got to have real conversations. The talks were mostly about boxing and basketball. The real heated argument started over politics and marriage topics. The barbershop played a fundamental role in the lives of young black boys; the barbershop was able to contribute to central issues structurally in the black community. The government and church couldn't primary affect the black men. Single-parent black women raising black boys would take them down to the barbershop—sometimes all day—to learn how to be a man. Eighty percent of my friends didn't have their fathers in the home—entire towns and neighborhoods fatherless. The black church became a lodging place for the single black mother to throw all their grievances on Jesus, thus this saying became popular: "I don't need a black man; all I need is Jesus." The black church played a huge role in the new reconstruction of the slaves; the problem was we didn't know this social construct was happening again. The feminist agenda celebrated the division between the black family; this gave the dominant society a strategical advantage. The State Department and Democratic Party created long-term damage that would last generations to come. The black women couldn't see the end goal of the State Department, to provide the bare necessities of housing, medicine, food, education, public safety, jobs, and judicial prudence while simultaneously destroying the institution of the family function. The irresistible bait wasn't obvious to black women; the State Department created the conditions for genocide using boards of education, guidance counselors, social services, and child welfare social workers from the State Department to bully black mothers by threatening to remove their children if they didn't remove their husbands. The system used every tool the state could leverage against black women. Utility companies and landlords created an apparatus of red tape and gerrymandering. The end goal was to replace black fathers with the government. The strong black woman weakened the black family. This idea of the autonomous black woman, commission by the State, brought a combination of behavioral characteristics and emotions such as resistance to co-parenting, irreconcilable differences, and opposition of compliance in marital roles. Things spiraled out of control for the black women who resisted the reconstruction of the black family and received domestic sanctions, penalties up to jail, loss of employment, housing defunding, rejection of community college, evictions, revoking of welfare benefits, and cancellation of utilities. The State Department dispatched private investigators to stake out the black community. This secret surveillance observed the black women's compliance. This avalanche of state control caused catastrophic damages; meanwhile, as the inner-city factories vanished mysteriously, steel mills, iron smelting plants, lumber mills, and cement industrial businesses—all the manufacturing industry—shipped overseas. The very engine of the American dream completely was gone; a new planogram was created. Since black men didn't have financial testicles, this economic castration allowed the government to place liquor stores on every corner of the black community. The last to go was the coal mining industry, which was gutted and shipped to China. By the early 1990s, the government-controlled drug program had completely desolated the black man. Crack cocaine and heroin had added to the black community's post-traumatic slave syndrome, which had never been treated. Our sickness mixed with chemicals we called food and drugs—a perfect formula paid for by the State Department and the scientists of America. My haircut was almost done. Some brothers from Jamaica and Nigeria were arguing about the transatlantic slave trade. Most African American usually didn't have much information on our African ancestry. The brothers were talking about some guy named Marcus Gravy and African unity. The conversation was nice, but I had to get back to the house. I wanted to hear more. The things they were saying made sense, but I didn't know how black people could come together. I learned a lot in the barbershop on why young black boys hated their fathers. We didn't know about the State Department or attorneys general and city hall removing our fathers; we just thought they'd left. Being black and gaining knowledge of the self is like watching a movie under a star projector; each decade is a smoke screen to mask the hidden framers. I made it home just before my mother; when she walked in the door, she spoke to everyone and told me to go into the back room. I was whipped for ten minutes with no clothes on. My Aunt Karen and my mother argued about the method of discipline. My mother told my Aunt Karen the house in Queens was ready; the only thing we were waiting on was the utility company to turn on our lights. I liked the Bronx. There were so many things to do. After my beating, my punishment ended. It was a choice of sitting in the house for weeks with no television and snakes or the belt. The Bronx had a basketball little league program, but you had to live in the community. So I told my aunt about it, and she wrote the coach a letter explaining I'd lived with her and was away at school. This worked. The coaches knew all the kids in the community. I was supposed to be a backup, but two of the starters got arrested on drug charges. I wasn't much of a shooter, but I has an untouchable crossover and spinning layup. We made it to the championship and won off of that move. The coach wanted me to keep playing and go to school in the local district, so my Aunt Karen spoke to my mother about the offer. She agreed to it. The only problem was I had to live with my Aunt Karen. That worried my mother. She thought my Aunt Karen wasn't strict enough, but she finished the paperwork. I had three months to get ready and start training, and school after New Year's. My aunt had a little helper that went to the store for her and helped her around the house. Her name was Jessica. She was a tomboy. I hated her guts, and she had a big mouth. My aunt used her to keep an eye on what I was doing. Jessica loved basketball more than any kid I knew, and she loved wrestling. She was strong. My aunt and sister always hyped her up to wrestle me. Sadly, sometimes she'd win, and they would laugh. The strangest thing was that Jessica was beautiful but dressed like a boy, and she liked girls. People didn't know. They assumed she was just a tomboy. One day her older sister was looking for Jessica, and she came to the house. My aunt told her sister Jessica had gone to the Chinese restaurant to get some chicken wings and should be back in twenty minutes. My aunt made a joke that I was Jessica's boyfriend, which wasn't funny at all. My aunt was always putting the idea in our heads. I went outside, embarrassed. Her sister couldn't wait any longer, so she gave me a key to give to Jessica. her sister was going on a date with her boyfriend, and their mother was in the hospital.

She told me, "FYI, Jessica likes girls—don't get your hopes up." Jessica was Dominican and black. All of her family was beautiful, so that night my aunt made macaroni and cornbread to go with the Chinese chicken. My aunt kept hundreds of packets of Kool-Aid, mostly orange and lemon. My older sister and my aunt's older daughter hung out all the time, Keisha and Khadija. My baby sister, Danielle, had the Nintendo to herself, and my mother spent most of her time in the church in Brooklyn when she wasn't working or taking business, as it were. The cool thing about Jessica was that she liked to play basketball, so we'd sneak to the park to play one-on-one when my aunt would go to sleep, and I found a way to smoke weed without Jessica telling: as long as I played her, she wouldn't tell. We played for hours. Some games she'd win; some I would win. Jessica was sixteen and very shapely—the only time you could see was when she played ball and got sweaty. She was sexy on the court. One night she was doing laundry and washing her shorts. All she had were some spandex shorts to wear. We went to play basketball around 1:00 a.m.—that was the only time we didn't fight. I lost every game that night. Her butt was bouncing everywhere, and the sweat made watermarks, and all of her prints and curves were showing. Something very weird happened to us that night. Jessica never posted me up; she always shot and laid the ball up. This night, almost every possession she posted me up with her back toward me, and I got excited every time. It got to the point we both were missing every shot. Our clothes were drenched in so much sweat her pants became see-through. She talked so much smack. I was pissed. We left our Walkman in her hallway. Her house was three doors down from my Aunt Karen. I was so angry I planned to get my Walkman and then hit her in the head with the ball—not to hurt her, just so she'd close her mouth. We walked into her hallway. Once I grabbed my Walkman, I threw the ball. It bounced off her head lightly. I tried to run out the door, but the knob fell out of the door. She wanted to fight. We started wrestling. She threw some punches and ripped my shirt. I was getting tired and didn't know how this was going to end— maybe I'd made a big mistake. I slammed her against something on the floor.

She said, "Time—OK, stop," which was unusual for her. I didn't stop. She stopped fighting and got quiet. Finally I stopped. We both got up off the floor. One of our Walkmans was broken—that was what I had slammed her against. I could feel the broken pieces on the floor. Both of us were hurting. I couldn't see a thing except the light coming from the door. She was blocking the door. I tried reaching for the knob. Jessica had the knob in her hand, so now I had to fight to get the knob to get out of the hallway. I kept asking for the knob. I didn't want to fight anymore; plus, I felt bad she had hurt her back. Every time I asked for the knob, she said no. I must have asked thirty times. She wouldn't open the door or move. I could tell her pride was hurting the way she kept saying no; after a while, her breathing changed. I kept asking to leave. She started saying no differently. Her no kept pulling me closer to her; the last time she said no, I felt a tingling feeling. I told her to open the door. She said no. I said no. We kept saying no until we started kissing. She dropped the knob; the sweat in her hair and underarms smelled so good. We kissed until the horizon started. I took her virginity that night. I tiptoed into the house. My aunt was sitting at the window. She watched me walk into the house. I slept on the sofa.

She asked me one thing: "Where is Jessica? In the house?" I said yes and went to sleep. The next morning Jessica came to the house wearing a dress and slippers. My aunt sent her to the store to get pancakes and a half cart of eggs and some milk. My aunt asked me, "What do you do to Jessica?"

I said, "Nothing."

She said, "Whatever, boy. You know you like her."

I said, "No way."

We skipped a couple of nights playing basketball and went to her house to watch wrestling. We both were big WWF fans. Jessica loved Hulk Hogan. My guy was the Undertaker. Every Saturday night we watched wrestling together. One morning my mother told me to get dressed, and we took a train to Queens to wait for the utility company. The lights came on around 6:00 p.m. My mother told me to watch television until she got back. She said she was going to get some groceries. After about five hours, my mother returned with my sisters. My mom had gone to the Bronx and come back. I was waiting to go back to the Bronx. Jessica was all I could think about. My mother wanted me to stay in Queens until it was time to go to school. My aunt kept telling her to bring me back so I could practice with the summer school team, but she said no. Jessica was pregnant. I didn't know it; my aunt did. The only one Jessica told was my Aunt Karen. My mother sent me to the store to get a two-liter Pepsi, five peppermints, and some lunch meat. I walked to the corner store. There was a dice game going on in front of the store; at least thirty people in front of the store were smoking and freestyle rapping. I stopped to watch. One guy passed me a blunt, and some of the homeys told me to grab a cup and pour some E&J. They didn't know me. Everybody assumed I was with one of the OGs. This was my first time standing on the corner. I had only seen this in rap videos—this was cool. I went back to the house. My mother had just left to go to church. Thank God. I smelled like weed and alcohol. My mother and older sister had gotten into a fight. My younger sister, Danielle, told me my mother had found out Keisha had a boyfriend. After my mother left, Keisha was like our second mother and babysitter. Maybe she didn't get to enjoy her childhood because of us. Little did I know that would be my last time seeing my sister for years. She ran away and had a baby, which made my mother mad, but the show must go on. Danielle and I went with my mother to church every Sunday, sometimes on Wednesdays; other nights we stayed home until my mother got back, sometimes two days. I started selling drugs in the first week of living in Queens; it was a revolving door, with so many young boys going in and out of jail and so many beautiful young girls using crack. After six months of selling crack cocaine, I didn't want to go back to the Bronx or play basketball for the school anymore. The FBI and CIA were watching our every move and had undercover cops all around the community. My older sister would come to the house when my mother wasn't there. Keisha was street smart; she knew I was selling drugs and was very disappointed in me. Every time she came, I was outside. I changed so much. My mother didn't know about my underworld dealings. I concealed my lifestyle; plus, my mother was chasing her dreams to become a pastor and worked part time, and she went to school at night.

Being in a single-parent home made it easy for me to have free time to become grown overnight. I couldn't trust anybody around me between government informants and snitches—the drug game was so dangerous. I couldn't believe so many young high school and college girls were using heroin and crack. Whenever they didn't have the money, they just performed sexual favors. I was guilty of this. I had a car in three months that I parked away from my house. One of the young boys who had started dealing around the same time as I had was arrested and needed a ride back to the block. He got out in just four hours and sent me a page on my beeper and didn't want me to tell our boss because once you go to jail, nobody trusts you anymore. He took a plea deal and got probation. I waited for him for nearly forty-five minutes; after waiting so long, I parked and went inside to see what was taking him so long. I walked into a courtroom and sat down for two hours just watching the cases. Every black male was sentenced to jail or probation. I didn't realize how much time had gone by. No parents were showing up for these young juveniles delinquents. I was speechless and walked out into the hallway. My friend Larry was talking with two white men. He was still in handcuffs. They took the cuffs off and shook his hand. I ran back to my car. I realized this was one big operation. The police weren't trying to catch us. They already had us. The young guys like us dealt with the local police detectives; the bosses dealt with the FBI; the drug lords dealt with the CIA. It was all a game or business. Larry got in the car. I asked him, "What took you so long?" He said he was waiting for his release papers. Larry asked me how many drugs I had on me; he said he had a customer. I said, "Wait, how? You just got out."

Larry was confused and said the customer had called him. Larry kept asking me how many packs of drugs I was moving in a day, and he was naming some people to have me agree with him. I told him my tooth was hurting, so he stopped asking questions. Later that day a drug sweep of the entire community happened. All the head drug dealers got out of Dodge; van loads of black men were arrested; five drug houses were raided. The only reason I wasn't swept up in the raid was that a female invited me to her house. I went to the pay phone to call my boss' he told me to stay off the block for the week, and the police went to his house. When I got off the phone, a policeman told me to put my hands behind my back in front of the barbershop. I had nothing on me, and they still arrested me. The community was very angry. I had become popular, young, and handsome. The police took me to central booking, then Rikers Island. I never got to see the judge. They loaded me up on a bus going to C-76; that was where the adolescents were taken on Rikers. The state gave me a lawyer, who met with me the next day. He told me the state had a good case. They had money and a direct sale I had made that day. He said he could get me home if I took six months and five years' probation. The lawyer told me my court date was two weeks from that day. My lawyer came back two more times to offer me different plea bargains. I refused them all. My court date came up, and I was remanded again without seeing the judge. My lawyer came to see me before I was sent back to Rikers Island; the young white man, my lawyer, told me the DEA wanted to see my parents and set my court date for three weeks from that day—that was the only way I could be released. The lawyer told me the judge was about to sign the new order, but he could probably get me out today if I took a plea of time served and five years; probation. I told the lawyer, "I'll take it—just get me out of here." Sure enough, the lawyer came back with good news and told me I'd be released that night at midnight. I got back on the bus going back to Rikers Island, and my father sat right in front of me. My father didn't recognize me. I called his name. When he turned around and saw me, tears came to his eyes. He was locked up for using crack cocaine, and myself for selling crack cocaine. I had never met my father's side of the family or known where he was staying, so he gave me the number to his sister's house, my aunt Beverly. I memorized the number. That was the last time I would see him for many years. I went home that night. They released me around 1:30 a.m. I went back to the block. My car had been towed, and my mother and sister weren't home. Everything at home was the way I had left it. My window wasn't locked, but the lights were turned off, and the food was spoiled in the refrigerator. I didn't want to sell drugs anymore, but I needed money to get my car or another one. My mother and sister never did return. Mom got married to a preacher she had been dating for years. I had always thought the red limo the preacher was driving that was parked outside of our house was a taxi. My mother and sister moved in with him; he lived in a better neighborhood and took care of my mother and sister. I went back to selling drugs. It's the same as prostitution. Whether you know it or not, the street itself is the drug. The drug game was worse than the music business. It was like a transportation terminal—no success could come from it. Young people were stuck in a never-ending story. We didn't understand as young people that life was more important and bigger than girls, drinking, fun, gold chains, and rap songs. We were helping the system with population control. We as young people thought the police were the problem; we didn't know about Congress passing laws to incarcerate the black male. I went to Manhattan the next morning to meet with my probation officer. Her name was Ms. Jones. There were three people ahead of me, so I went outside to get a coffee and jelly doughnut. While I waited in line, some kleptomaniac grabbed this white man's wallet and ran. The man didn't even notice his wallet had been taken. I don't know what got into me. I chased the man down, yelling, "Stop! He stole my wallet!" The man dropped the wallet and kept running. I picked up the wallet and opened it to see the name of the person. It belonged to Bobby Bianchi. He was an older Italian man. He was a union guy, Local 295. I gave the wallet back to the man. He offered me fifty bucks. The man at the concession stand gave me my coffee and doughnut for free. I didn't take the money. As soon as I walked back into the Department of Corrections. It was my turn. I put my doughnut in my pocket and took a sip of the coffee, then through it in the trash. I couldn't believe Ms. Jones was a PO; she was twenty-three years old and fine.

She went over the rule and told me for the first three months report to the machine. "Don't break my trust. Now get out of my office." I walked out that office feeling great. I planned to sell drugs for six more months, then get a job. Ms. Jones called me by my last name. She said, "Let me show you how to use this machine." She was leaving for the day. We walked out the door together. She told me, "Stay away from police and weed, and you'll be fine." I walked her to the car. Ms. Jones offered to take me home, so I got in her car. She was driving a BMW. Before we took off, the man I had helped get his wallet back knocked on the window. I rolled the window down.

He handed me a card and said, "My name is Bobby. If you need a job, call me."

Ms. Jones said, "Wow," laughing. "That's a first." She said, "Are you hungry?" We went through Wendy's drive-through. She turned the radio on. It was on AM 1010. I switched the station to WLBS-FM. Usher was playing "Superstar." Ms. Jones said, "I want you to call that man and start working so you have money for transportation." She said, "I normally don't do this, but take my home phone number. Call me and tell me what you need for work after you speak to the man. OK, now get out." She dropped me off in front of my home. I took the food in the house and walked straight to the pay phone.

On the third ring, Bobby answered the phone and said, "Meet me at the Copacabana tomorrow at seven a.m." and hung up the phone.

When I got back to the house, Ms. Jones was waiting in front of the house. "I forgot my drink." I told her Bobby had offered me a job tomorrow at 7:00 a.m. Ms. Jones told me to get in her car. She took me to a men's store and brought me two suits, a pair of shoes, and a watch. My life was in the toilet bowl, but God always has a plan. She drove me back home. I put my seat back and turned up her radio. She didn't say a word. She knew I was a street nigga and just needed a little support. She stopped in front of the house. She said, "I believe in you. Call me anytime, and stay out of trouble." Ms. Jones was studying to be a judge. She didn't have any friends or children. She was divorced. Her only responsibility was her mother and her cats. I thank God for her—she felt like a guardian angel. Her family was from Trinidad. She was still an island girl. The lights in the house were off. It was hard to see. I still had $200 worth of crack cocaine in dimes. I walked to a store blocks away from my community to avoid the streets. A crackhead noticed me and asked if I had some work on me. He had a guy who needed $500 worth. I brought my candle and gave him my $200 and ran to the house. I promised never to sell another drug again. In just a year, I had made $2 million, and almost all the money had gone to my boss. Drug dealing wasn't worth my freedom. I got up early the next morning, around 5:30, and took the train to Manhattan to meet with Bobby. I stopped to get a coffee with a bagel and cream cheese. The Copacabana wasn't far from the subway. I got off at Forty-Second street and took a taxi. I'm an early bird, plus my new suit looked good on me. I wanted everybody to see how nice the kid was when he cleaned up. The place was classy. When I got to the front entrance, the security told me to go through the kitchen. Bobby didn't know he was doing me a big favor. He told me I looked great and next time to wear some black tennis shoes. I delivered food for eight hours straight. I didn't even take a lunch my first three days. At the end of the week, Bobby gave me $600. My first two months, I made $7,000. There were three other delivery boys, Pauly, Vinnie, and Mikey. I was the only black kid in the whole joint. I reported to Ms. Jones on time for three years faithfully, and every year my money doubled. Some days I cooked in the kitchen and washed dishes. I spent most of my time with old Italian men; they loved me. On my seventeenth birthday, Bobby brought me a car. The guys joked he was my dad. Bobby didn't have any kids, and his wife had died. She was a black woman. They were married for thirty years. Mikey and I got a place together in New Jersey, twenty minutes from the Copacabana. The Italians had a rule: no selling drugs. They got me out of the ghetto. Every weekend Pauly, Mikey, Vinnie, and I partied in Atlantic City. One night I drove up to the Bronx to see my Aunt Karen; she was sitting in the same place, the window. When I got out of the car, she thought she saw a ghost, by the look in her eyes. I had no regrets about not coming back to the Bronx. It wasn't my decision. Once I started selling drugs, basketball was no longer important. The income changed my outcome. I gave my Aunt Karen a nice big hug and kiss.

The first thing she said to me was "Go to the store and get me some cigarettes." On my way to the store, I thought about stopping by to see Jessica. Maybe she was at the basketball court.

I asked my aunt if it was OK to spend the night. "Tomorrow's my day off." We talked about two hours about my life and goals. I even told Aunt Karen about my bad habit of selling drugs, jail, and probation. It had been almost a year. She hadn't heard from my mother. My mom was like that with everyone. Now you see her; now you don't. It wasn't personal, just business with her. My aunt was proud of me for working so hard down at the Copacabana, earning an honest living after selling drugs and all. We talked until she started yawning.

Right after, she said, "When are you going to see Jessica?"

I told my aunt. "Don't start the Jessica and me thing again."

My aunt asked me, "Did you know Jessica had a baby?"

I was surprised but not jealous. "Wow, didn't see that one coming." She told me to go see her, and she handed me Jessica's baby bag that she had left over at the house. My aunt told me she was the babysitter in the mornings while Jess worked, so I walked next door and knocked on the door. Some Spanish chick with an attitude answered the door and said, "What is it?"

I handed her the bag and said, "Jessica left the bag over at my Aunt Karen's house." Jessica heard my voice and opened the door.

She apologized; she said, "That's my girlfriend. Don't mind her."

I said, "Girlfriend like in a relationship?"

She said, "Yeah." Jessica's baby was sleeping in her crib; she asked me if I would like to hold the baby. It was time to feed her.

I said, "Sure, why not?" Jessica gave me the baby and sat down, watching to make sure I was holding the baby correctly. The baby was beautiful. She opened her eyes twice. Once she took a good look at me, she started crying.

Jessica said, "Give me the baby." While I was handing her the baby, she took her shirt off and pulled her bra up and fed the baby in front of me. Her girlfriend grabbed their car keys and walk out the door. Jessica walked behind her, asking, "When will you be back?" Her girlfriend got in the car and took off. When Jessica came back, she continued to feed the baby. She fully removed her bra and said, "Your baby is two years old." Immediately I thought back to that night we had sex. She had turned the radio on that night to listen to *The Quiet Storm*. "Juicy Fruit," by Mtume, was the third song to play that night. I remember it well because we made the baby to that song.

All I could do was cry. "My baby girl, your daddy missed your birth." Jessica and my Aunt Karen had tried to contact me and told my mother about the baby, but she didn't believe it. I told Jessica, "I'm so sorry. Please forgive me." She gave the baby back to me. We took the baby to my Aunt Karen's house three doors down. She was sitting in the window smiling.

My aunt said, "Bring that baby here." Her name was Savannah. My aunt watched Savannah. She sent us to the store to get two packs of cigarettes. She told me to pay now that I was a working man. We walked and caught up on so many things, including her relationship, which was now the rocks. She said they fought too much. My whole life had changed in just a few hours. Jessica and I still had a fire. I could tell by the way she kept looking at me. I remember those looks. Just like that, I wanted her so bad. Somebody drove by our block bumping some "Computer Love." I had planned to spend the night. Now I was thinking about moving back to the Bronx to be closer to my baby and my aunt. I walked Jessica and Savannah back to the house; it brought back so many memories of that special night. We had also fought in that hallway. As soon as I walked into the hallway, I noticed they had fixed the doorknob. The passion was so strong in that place that we started kissing again. The neighbors upstairs were jamming some Midnight Star, "Feels So Good." Jessica stopped me from kissing her. She said I had to go and come back tomorrow, or she would bring the baby to my aunt's house. My aunt was sitting in the window. She didn't say a word. I walked slowly toward her and sat on the porch thinking. Early the next morning, I took Savannah and Jessica to IHOP. We talked about co-parenting and respecting each other's boundaries. We decided to be friends and share everything as long as I moved back to the Bronx. I agreed. We shook hands and took the baby for some ice cream. I got strawberry; Jessica got chocolate; Savannah got to share with us. We spent the entire day together; by the time we got home, it was midnight. My Aunt Karen was sitting in the window, as usual being nosy. Her smile could not have been more obvious. She was happy to see us together. Jessica's girlfriend, on the other hand, was furious that Savannah was in my arms. Jessica was holding the bags of clothes and boxes of Pampers I had brought for Savannah when we went inside the house before. I put the baby down. Jessica and Sabrina got into a fistfight. She ripped Jessica's shirt completely off her. She wasn't wearing a bra. The shirt said I Love My Family. I took my baby with me to my aunt's house and stayed out of their business. After one hour I went back to check if the lovebirds had finished horseplaying. They were taking a nap. The door was cracked the way had I left it. The house was a mess, but they were sleeping peacefully. The baby was hungry, so I brought Savannah home. They woke up when they heard her crying. Jessica got out of the bed and got the baby and apologized.

I told her, "No need." Sabrina walked into the living room with no clothes on and sat right next to Jessica on the sofa. I just left. She had done that on purpose to make me jealous. It worked. I went back to work. All I could think about was Savannah. Eventually my goal was to move back to the Bronx, but it would be wise if I made the transition slowly. For months I commuted from Manhattan to the Bronx. Every time I came over to see Savannah, Sabrina purposely walked around naked. She was a very thick white girl with a DD chest and a huge butt. I was attracted and angry at the same time. One night when the baby was sleeping in the other room, I dropped off some things for Savannah. Jessica was wearing a towel, and Sabrina was naked. Sabrina purposely started wrestling with Jessica and turned her upside down and carried her around the room, both with no clothes. I dropped the clothes and money on the floor and left. I stayed away for two weeks. Sabrina's plan had worked. I didn't give up my place in New Jersey. Early one morning I drove out to the Bronx to take Jessica and Savannah to IHOP so we could talk. I called first from my Aunt Karen's house.

Jessica said, "Sure, come to pick us up." When I got to the door, she opened it with no clothes.

I said, "What is it with y'all and no clothes?"

Jess laughed and said, "All women are like that. They like to be free." Jessica said, "Let me wake the baby up." I asked her where her girlfriend was. She said they were taking some time to cool off—the fights were becoming too much, especially with a baby in the house. Savannah was sleeping in her little Pampers. Jessica was playing some Selena, "Como la flor," and folding the baby's clothes. Selena was Jessica's favorite singer. She grabbed me by my shirt to the middle of the floor to dance with her. I loved bachata. We danced to Monchy & Alexandra's "Hoja en blanco." We made love right in the middle of the floor while dancing. Jessica was a freak. I loved it when she called me "*papi.*" The baby woke up. We kept going. I could feel we loved each other with a real passion. We danced and made love on and off for nearly one hour. I was in love with Jessica, the only man to make love to her, and we had a child together. We never used protection, and we knew better. We took a shower together. Baby Savannah woke up, and we went to eat at IHOP. This time we took Aunt Karen with us. Jessica and I both loved being parents. Our relationship was complicated. At first Sabrina bothered me, as did the fact that Jessica liked girls. But the more I talked to my Aunt Karen and thought about it, Jessica was perfect. Sabrina had come out of nowhere. She wasn't from the hood. She was a German college student from upstate New York. Something about Sabrina was weird. Even Jessica said that every time I came around, she got very upset, and Jessica told me she played these crazy mind games. I had one last visit to my probation officer, and Jessica and I discussed the possibility of living together. After we dropped off Aunt Karen, Jessica and I watched Savannah sleep. Jessica noticed Savannah slept better when I was around. Jessica asked me to spend the night and sleep on the sofa. Jessica played some nice bachata and poured some wine. I helped her light their fireplace. She made a nice bed on the floor out of thick blankets and pillows. We made love in front of the fire for hours, and Savannah slept through the night. Jessica and I kept telling each other, "Sorry. I love you." We made passionate love all night. The fire felt great on our bare skin. Early in the morning, I left to go see Ms. Jones. I had to be at work at 1:00 p.m. I arrived at her office at 9:00 a.m. after getting my usual coffee and doughnut. Ms. Jones was good about letting me get in and out. She respected my time. She took my last urine sample and gave me my discharge papers. She gave me a hug and an invitation to eat with her and her mother at the Cracker Barrel in Staten Island at 8:00 p.m. Ms. Jones told me to call her Monica. She said she hated being called Ms. Jones—it made her feel old. I left the job at 6:45 to give myself time to get there just in case of traffic. I found a parking place in the busy parking lot. Monica and her mother were seated already. When I walked in, Monica saw me right away and waved me over. I walked over to the table where Monica and her mother were sitting. Her mom looked so familiar. Monica introduced us. She told her mother my name, and her mother's name was Ms. Virginia.

I said, "Please excuse me" and ran to the bathroom. Her mother was the woman in the bookstore, Ms. Virginia. I put some water on my face and went back out to the table and sat down.

I was so nervous. Monica asked me if was I OK. Her mother said, "He's just fine." She said, "Did Monica tell you about my husband, her father? You look just like him. His name is Hank." I took a sip of the water at the table and choked.

Monica said, "You do look just like my dad. That's why I want my mother to see you." Monica had said she told her mother everything about her work because her mother was her best friend. I wanted ask about the bookstore, but I was afraid Monica's mother was wearing the same necklace, which read "Pangaea," from the bookstore. We ate and told jokes. Ms. Virginia had a great sense of humor and gorgeous eyes. Monica was so beautiful. She was wearing an all-black dress with black shoes and black lipstick; her natural hair was so nice. The food was great. I had chicken fried steak with white gravy and mixed vegetables. Monica and Ms. Virginia had seafood platters. Monica had the waiter bring a surprise birthday cake. Monica and her mother wished me a happy belated birthday. I celebrated two weeks again with my roommates. Pauly was leaving with me and Mikey. My roommates helped me get through so many sleepless nights. Monica gave me a nice watch and a bottle of cologne for my birthday. Ms. Virginia gave me a white envelope, and I opened it; inside was a round-trip ticket to Egypt and a two-dollar bill. Monica had no idea what her mother was doing. Monica was supposed to take her mother to Egypt, but her mother was sick and asked me to go. Monica apologized to me and said, "You don't have to go." I told her I wanted to go. Monica was getting ready to take her mother home. I asked Monica to join me for a latte. She said no at first, but I begged her for just twenty minutes. She agreed. I took her to the Copacabana; it was old-school (seventies and eighties) night. Mikey was at the door. Vinnie and Pauly was working the kitchen. I took Monica through the kitchen. We tasted some of the food I introduced Monica to my boss, Bobby. She said, "That's the guy that gave you a job three years ago. Monica was surprised the way the Italians treated me like one of their own. I was a part of the family. The Ronettes were playing "Be My Baby" (1963). I was surrounded by older Italian men. Bobby made sure we had the best champagne. I could tell Monica was happy. The music was perfect. She love the Jersey Boys' "Sherry"; it was one of her mother's favorites songs. Bobby had paid for a room at the Waldorf Astoria; on our way out, he told us. He said the room was for his uncle, who had gotten stuck in New Jersey working. Monica was ready to go home. We had had a great time. We walked outside to a white stretch limousine, compliments of the family. Monica and I just looked at each other. She said, "I'm crazy. I've never been to the Waldorf Astoria. I'll just stay for twenty minutes. Deal?"

I said, "Deal" and got inside the limousine. The driver was playing Martha Reeves's "Jimmy Mack." I couldn't believe it. We opened another bottle of champagne. We both drank a glass.

Monica asked me, "What do you do for work?"

I said, "I sell pizza." We laughed and drank another glass. The room and hotel had beautiful rose petals everywhere. Bobby was married to a black woman for many years. He had set the perfect mood. A record player was in the room. A classic Anita Baker record, *Giving You the Best That I Got*, was on the track. Monica put the needle on the record. She turned the lights down. We danced our way into love. We left around 3:00 a.m. We left a nice tip and the room nice. The limo took us back to our cars.

Monica got in her car and said, "Good night. Thank you." I watched her drive away. I took my vacation time for our trip to Egypt. I'd never been out of the country. Before we left, I spent time with Jessica and Savannah. Sabrina had come back in the picture. Jessica told Sabrina that I needed a place, and the both of them wanted to speak with me. Sabrina and Jessica wanted to know if I would have a polygamous relationship with them. I wasn't thrilled about the idea at first. Jessica made sure Savannah was sleeping. The three of us drunk red wine (two bottles). I had a flight to catch in the morning with Monica. Sabrina kept pouring me more wine. While we were talking, Sabrina took her clothes off and helped Jessica take her clothes off to. Now I was more confused. Sabrina kissed Jessica below in front of me, and Jessica let her. That night I had my first threesome. It was amazing. I don't remember much about that night but in the middle of the threesome, I remember seeing that Sabrina had a tattoo of the planet Saturn on the back of her neck and that Jessica had a tattoo of the yin and yang; the same symbols that were on Diana and Mommy were on Jessica and Sabrina. I woke up early the next morning and drove to New Jersey, showered, and got ready for my flight. I was supposed to meet Monica at JFK airport. I made it right on time. Monica was at the airport four hours early. She told me I didn't have to do this. She said, "I feel like my mother made you go."

SABRINA, JESSICA, MONICA, SAVANNAH

I explained to Monica: "This was a birthday gift from your mother and a dream come true for me, and I would like to spend it with you." Monica had set up a tour guide. When we landed at Cairo Airport, the man was holding a sign with Monica's name on. It he took us to our hotel. Monica suggested we get another room so I could feel free to enjoy myself. Ms. Virginia and Monica were supposed to have shared a room with two separate beds. We agreed the one room was good enough. The first night, we had dinner and rode on some camels. The second day, we went to the pyramids and the Valley of the Kings, and the third night we stayed in Alexandria. On the fourth night, we went to a dinner party off the Nile River. We were having so much fun, like little kids. On our fifth day, we ordered some food and shopped locally. We told the tour guide to take the day off. We just wanted to chill. We made love the whole day. We both couldn't wait. I loved this woman. I asked her to marry me on the hot desert sand. I told her everything about myself, including Jessica, Sabrina, work, Savannah.

Monica said, "You don't understand, do you?" Monica said I wasn't ready and I had more important things to deal with. Me and my big mouth. I think I scared her away. Someone knocked on the door. I opened the door. It was the tour guide

He said to Monica, "We're ready, Your Highness."

Monica told him, "We'll be down in five minutes."

The tour guide said, "Andromeda is waiting for you, Your Highness." I looked at both of them like, what is this "Your Highness" business? I had no idea what or where we were going. At eleven o'clock at night, Monica changed her clothes to an all-black catsuit with black boots and black sunglasses; she had clothes waiting for me to change into, all black with sunglasses. She said something about not being able to travel without wearing black. We walked outside and got into a black truck. I assumed maybe we were going dancing. The driver and tour guide were wearing all black. We were taken to the Great Pyramid. The cornerstone had been removed from the top of the Great Pyramid. I started to wonder what was going on.

Monica told me it was a surprise; she said, "Don't be afraid." A bright light covered the top of the hole where the cornerstone was. The light beamed down on me once the cornerstone was removed. I was beamed up to a ship called *Andromeda*. I was completed paralyzed. The black women on the ship removed my pupils and replaced them with new ones and added some devices to my eardrums. There was a mirror on the ceiling of the ship. The mirror was like liquid. They removed my wisdom teeth and added new ones. When the women finished operating on me, they marked my right arm with two dots. Monica closed my eyes. I woke up the next morning. My body was so hot, and my sheet was soaking wet. I already knew it had been a bad dream. Monica was sleeping. Our trip had changed so many things about my outlook on life. I didn't want to spoil things with my crazy dreams. There was a knock on the door. I was a little cautious until I heard "room service." It was breakfast. Monica woke and went into the bathroom as the waiter set up our food. She looked so good in the morning—black silk lingerie with her natural hair in a ponytail. I tipped the waiter, and he left. The shower was on in the bathroom, so I knocked on the door to tell Monica the food was ready. She said, "OK, baby, I'm coming." My relationship with Monica was different the more time we spent together. I liked her and loved her. My love was based on logical structure. When Monica came out of the bathroom, I know that that was my wife. Her fingers and toenails were painted black, and her lipstick was black. We spent our last days in Egypt doing local things and talking about our future. I didn't think much about Jessica on the flight home. We talked about her mother and childhood. Her story was amazing. As an only child, she had felt lonely most of her life. Her mother had told her she could see great things happening between us. Monica carried a phone with a picture of her father with her on it. I asked to see it. The man looked like my twin—a little creepy. We slept the rest of the flight home leaning on each other. When we got back to JFK Airport, I picked up my car. Monica didn't drive. She took a taxi. We made back to her place a little past midnight. She invited me to sleep on the sofa because it was late. Monica and I were too tired. We went straight to sleep. She woke me up on the sofa and told me to get in the bed with her. We made love for ten minutes and went back to sleep. We got out of bed at nearly 2:00 p.m. We ate lunch and made love and went back to sleep. We did the same thing all day, and it felt good to rest and make love; both of us worked the next morning. Monica's house was very nice and peaceful. She had no movies, records, or games, just a library of books. Monica told me her love of books came from her mother, who used to be a librarian. She asked me if I liked to read. That was a tough question to answer because it wasn't something I had ever done, but it sounded great. With the right opportunity, I was sure I would. I learned something very important being with Monica: the right woman makes life rich and rewarding, like being in heaven. We needed each other. Monica was willing to help me grow, and I learned so many things from her. She never intimidated me. She only empowered me from day one. I had so many things to think about, like my baby girl, Savannah, and my living arrangements. Maybe I was moving too fast. But to me, when you find that special person, the speed at which the relationship develops isn't scary. I went to work the next morning feeling responsible, happy, mature, and full of energy. It wasn't easy getting back in the swing of things—back to work was almost as bad when I was a kid going back to school after the winter recess. I started spending all my time with Monica. She was cleanly organized with perfect hygiene, and her goals in life pushed me to rethink what I wanted out of life. I partially moved in with Monica. We shared expenses and bills. Monica loved to read. She would read a book to me almost every day. I just listened and used my imagination. The books opened up my mind to a much different world from the one I lived in. Before Monica, relationships with me were based on sex, food, kids, and church—what materials one was exposed to was what one built with. I had never known love before, then came Monica. I started reading some of Monica's law books and studying them. I realized nothing in this world works the way we think it does. I also figured out that the more you read, the better your conversation is. I kept wondering why my past relationships were so hard to communicate. The next morning I showed up two hours earlier to work than normal. Bobby was in the kitchen getting things ready for the day; he did have to be to work this early. Bobby had never missed a day of work in ten years. When he saw me getting ready for work, he told me to sit down and poured me a cup of coffee. He asked me how were things going. Bobby said that when a man shows up early to work, either his life at home is very good or very bad—which one was it for me? I needed a stiff drink. Bobby was right, and he was the only father figure I had. He said things weren't as bad as they seemed. I told Bobby everything.

He told me my problem was that I wasn't honest with myself. Bobby said, "Just tell both women you're in love with them." Bobby told me, "Every man has two great ones in his life. Marry both—one on paper, and the other in the womb. Now get to work, kid." Bobby was right. After work I drove up to the Bronx. Jessica was sitting on the porch talking to my Aunt Karen with her sister. Jessica's sister was living with her boyfriend. Tina said that moving back home with Jessica was a good thing for Jessica. I parked the car and walked over to my aunt's place. The first thing my aunt did was send me to the store to get some cigarettes. I asked Jessica to walk with me to the store. I told Jess my trip to Egypt had been amazing. Everything I said went in one ear and out the other. She wasn't listening. Jessica didn't respond to the things I was talking about; then she just told me she and Sabrina broke up. I didn't care. Monica brought me balance; then Jessica told me she was pregnant again. She got more beautiful every time she got pregnant. I kissed her on her juicy Dominican lips. We gave the cigarettes to my aunt and asked them to watch Savannah for an hour while we went for a ride and talked. We drove to the nearest hotel and ripped each other's clothes off in the hallway. Her long black curly hair and beautiful caramel skin with pink lips made me put a baby in her every time.

Just before, I asked her, "Whose is it?"

She said, "Yours, poppy. Spank me. I've been a bad girl, poppy." Jessica told me she loved me. I told her about Monica and that we had talked about getting married. Jess said, "What about us? Me and you."

I thought about what Bobby told me, so I asked Jessica, "Could the three of us talk?" I asked Monica the same thing; they both agreed. My problem now was what was I going to say? Bobby was going to have to help with this one. I went home for the first time in a long time. The guys were surprised to see me. Both women were pulling on my brain and heart. I loved them both. I brought an engagement ring from the jewelry store. The next morning I went to Monica's house at 6:00 a.m. She was sleeping. I had the key to her apartment and started breakfast.

Monica woke up to the smell of the food. She called out, "Babe, is that you?"

I replied, "Yes, honey. Hungry?" To that, she said yes. I brought her breakfast in bed. The ring was under the pancakes. When she saw the ring, she cried and said yes. I made love to her warm morning. I went to work and told Bobby what was going on. After work he took me and some guys to the bowling alley. Bobby said I was in deep, but I was in. Now was not the time to start lying—that's for sure. He said I was fishing in a speedboat.

Bobby said that the man who hurts the woman the most is the one she loved the most. Bobby was deep and had so much wisdom. I could sure use him at the meeting with Monica and Jessica. After a few beers, Bobby's words made more sense. His words were like a golden apple, beautiful and valuable. I called the ladies to confirm. Monica was skeptical and asked what this was about. There was no turning back now. My aunt and Jessica's sister watched Savannah. Our meeting was at 6:00 p.m. tomorrow, on Friday night. That morning my worst nightmare happened. Monica called me to tell me her mother had passed away. We canceled our meeting. Monica was heartbroken. I used two sick days to spend with Monica, to comfort her. Ms. Virginia was all she had. We made the funeral arrangements and contacted her family. On the day of the funeral, Monica introduced me to her family. They came from all over the country. Monica and I grew closer. We sat together in the front row. The family buried Ms. Virginia and gave her a nice going-home service. After the family all came to support Monica at her home, I stayed close by her side. Monica put the necklace on that her mother used to wear. Monica asked her family to celebrate her mother's passing, not to mourn her, so we ate and danced. The positive vibes felt good, like Ms. Virginia was with us. I thought the time was right. I asked Monica to marry tomorrow; then we planned the wedding. She said yes. Monica said it was Ms. Virginia's last wish. She had told her I was the one. The next morning we went down to the justice of the peace and applied for the license. Three days later the courts married us. Bobby was my witness, and Monica asked her mother's younger sister to be a witness. She signed for us and went back to Texas. We planned to have our wedding celebration at the Copacabana the next month; things would take time to get back to normal. Even though we had celebrated her mother's life, the pain was real. Jessica's belly was getting bigger. I never got the opportunity to tell Monica, so months later we agreed to meet again. I told Monica that Jessica was pregnant again. It had happened before out engagement and marriage. Monica asked why I hadn't tell her earlier. Before she could come up with her ideas about my intentions, I told her, "You're passed when I was gonna tell you."

Monica said, "Invite her and the baby over to the house tomorrow night." She said, "I love you." Jessica and Savannah came over. We ate and sat down in the living room. Monica had a big two-level home. Jessica told her the house was beautiful. Jess, like myself, lived in an apartment building. Monica asked Jessica if she wanted to see the upstairs and backyard. She took Jessica to see the house. Monica asked Jessica, "What are your goals?"

Jess said, "To go back to school and become a registered nurse." Jessica asked Monica, "What about you?"

She said, "I just became a lawyer and am on my way to becoming a judge, but at the time I'm a probation officer."

Jessica said, "Wow." After the tour, we all sat down and watched Savannah play. Jessica told Monica she was sorry for her loss of her mother.

Monica said, "Thank you, and let's get down to business. Do you love him?"

Jessica said, "Yes, I do."

Monica said, "You know he's my husband, right?

Jessica said, "Yes, and I'm his baby mother."

I was waiting to speak and afraid.

Monica said, "I'm here to protect my husband. Would you be willing to move with the children with us? The kids need space, and we must help you."

Jessica said, "Yes."

Monica said, "It's settled." Monica took Jessica back upstairs to show the space for her and the babies, two bedrooms and a full bathroom. I never said a word. There was no need. Jessica told her sister and my Aunt Karen. They were sad but happy that we had come to a good agreement for the children. Once we took Jessica back home, Monica and I drove home. The car was completely silent. I was scared to say anything.

Monica said, "Do you know why I did that? Let Jessica come stay with us?"

I said, "Why?"

She said, "She's in danger. Get her to the house as soon as possible." I asked Monica what she was talking about. She pulled the car over and told me that her mother was my guardian angel. Ms. Virginia had been following me my whole life. When my first solar landed, I was married to her. My name had been Hank. Monica told me Ms. Virginia and I had a child and that child was Monica. I couldn't believe my ears. Monica said that I was on my second solar return and was from the constellation Sirius the Dog Star. Monica said that once she told me my constellation name, my eyes and ear would open. At that point, I'd be able to speak of vibrational frequency. She said Sabrina had been sent to kill me by the god of Saturn, so she had gotten close to Jessica. "Your name is Anubis." My eyes and ear were burning like fire. I asked her what had she done to me. She said, "Open your eye."

I said, "I can't." It hurt.

Monica said, "Open your eyes." I did. Everything around me was in code. I could hear everybody's voice from miles away. Monica said, "Everything natural to the planet has codes. The unnatural things have no codes." I was able to see Jessica and my Aunt Karen, even hear them. Anyone in my memory bank, I could look into their lives for thirty seconds only. Monica said, "Our role on Pangaea is just a part we play."

I asked Monica, "Why is Saturn trying to kill me?" She said because I had the power to destroy the moon. Monica said, "The moon is a satellite that controls the humans on the planet. It's a communication system. The moon is a converter. It translates the messages from Saturn to what they call Earth—we know it to be Pangaea." Monica said, "We communicate differently than the agents from Saturn. They use the moon; we use the sun. The moon is their mothership the sun is our mothership the war between good and evil." Everything was starting to make sense.

I asked Monica, "So who is Jessica?"

Monica said, "She's your portal and a part of our constellation and my sister, eastern star."

I said, "Monica, who are you?"

She said, "Only I know that—so far your wife." Monica said, "If Saturn can turn Jessica into a death star, she'll die or kill you. Once she's changed, one or the other will happen. Jessica has no idea. She's asleep waiting for her grand rise to happen. We're all watching ourselves from our constellation." Monica said, "Welcome back."

I asked, "Will we see Ms. Virginia again?"

Monica said, "For sure. Once one leaves Pangaea, they must wait three years to return and be born again to you or someone else. She'll probably come looking for you. She won't remember you until one of us performs a grand rising. That's why we took you to Egypt. The ceremony must be done in the East. She was planning to see you again. At least she got to see you once."

I said, "It's all starting to make perfect sense now."

Monica said, "We must try to get her to the house this week. Sabrina will be back soon."

I asked, "Why doesn't Sabrina try to kill me?"

"She's not allowed until you're aware of the knowledge of self. Until then she must convince someone else to do it." Monica said, "There are thousands like Sabrina. They can tell if you're awake because your energy is so powerful. Even those asleep can tell there's something about you. Be careful. Her greatest power is sex. If you refuse her, she'll know when you see her. She looks different. We brought you to the mothership and made a few changes. Your eyes were replaced."

I said, "Wait a minute—that was real?"

She said, "Yes." The next morning I went to work. My eyes didn't see flesh anymore. That was the hardest part. Monica was right. Once you're awake, it's difficult to blend into society.

Bobby asked me, "How are things going?" I told him he was a genius. Everything he had told me worked like a charm. Bobby was OK. His codes were normal. I had amazing powers. Mostly everything I looked at didn't have a code. The food and industrial structures—even some of the animals—didn't have codes. I was beginning to understand that Saturn was turning the humans' world into an artificial mankind world. What we called technology was information coming from Saturn: television; phone books; religion; radio; schools; court; systems; games. All are guidance from Saturn. All are systems of control. All these systems could be summed up in one word (civilization). Amazing. Civilization is an artificial concept designed to look identical to nature; the matrix is a nice way of describing what Saturn is doing to humans on Pangaea. I went to see Jessica and Savannah that night. Her sister said she had gone for a walk with the baby to the store. I walked toward the store. Jessica and Savannah were walking toward me. Jessica's belly was so big and beautiful. I loved my baby mother. She walked right up to me and kissed me on my lips and said, "Where is our wife?"

I said, "Who are you talking about?"

She said, "Monica."

Monica and Jessica

Jessica said she liked my wife. "Her spirit is genuine, and she loves you enough to help your baby mother." That made me respect her. I told Jessica to pack her things that night and I would explain later. She did just what I asked her. We took all the babies' clothes and most of Jessica's. Before we left, Sabrina pulled up with two other females and one male in a caravan. I told Jessica not to say a word. Monica was right. Sabrina was a reptilian, and so were all of the people in the vehicle. I was able to communicate with Monica. Our thought were connected, and my wisdom teeth had been replaced on the mothership. We both had a little over a week of vacation. I told her to book a flight two days from today to Egypt for the four of us. I listened to the conversation between Tina and Sabrina. We told Jessica's sister we were going to the hotel.

Sabrina asked her, "What hotel?" Tina told her she thought the Holiday Inn. Sabrina left with her reptilian friends to search for us. We made our way to Queens. Monica booked the tickets. Monica, through vibrational frequency, said Jessica must go on her free will. When we got back to the house, Monica and I sat with Jessica and told her we had a gift for her early baby shower. Monica and I told Jessica we were taking her to Egypt in two days.

Jessica laughed and said, "You're joking, right? What about Savannah?"

Monica said, "She's coming too. It's only for three days."

Jessica looked surprised and happy. She said, "Yes, let's go." Jessica wanted to go home and get a few things and tell her sister the good news. I told her not to tell Tina and to trust me. She didn't understand but agreed. I convinced my old roommate to cover for me and paid Mikey $300 to work for me. Bobby called to make sure everything was OK. I told Bobby we were wedding planning.

He said, "You kids have fun." Days later we bored our flight on time and made it safely to Egypt. Savannah was well behaved, and Jessica didn't have any trouble flying. We all sat near one another and talked about new living arrangements. Monica and Jessica joked that I had tricked them into living together because I wanted two women. Monica made the same plans with the tour guide and hotel. After all, our trip was so short on our first day that we went to the pyramids and the Nile River. On the second night, Monica and I dressed in black and picked out a nice black leather suit for Jessica. We even dressed baby Savannah in black. There was a knock on the door. Jessica opened the door.

The tour guide said to me, "Andromeda is waiting for Your Highness."

I said, "We'll be down in five minutes." We went down and got in a black truck and drove to the Great Pyramid. Monica, Jessica, Savannah, and I went inside. The cornerstone was removed. Jessica stood right in the middle where the cornerstone was removed. A beam of light came down so bright I couldn't see anything for five minutes, just codes. To Monica and I, Jessica was on the mothership only five minutes, but to her, it would feel like hours. We took Jessica back to the hotel. She was unconscious. Jessica completed her grand rising. Her knowledge of self would take a few days. The next morning Jessica woke up to a knock on the door; it was room service. Monica hopped in the shower, and I went in the bathroom to take a pee. Jessica knocked on the door to tell us the food was ready. I came out of the bathroom first, with my black boxers and a black T-shirt. Monica was wearing black panties and a black bra with black lipstick and black nails covered with a black robe. Jessica told us she had had a weird dream. I could tell she was starting. Our constellation was forming. On our last day in Egypt, we took Savannah and Jessica shopping. We spent the last night in Egypt doing local things.

When we got back to the room, Monica kissed me in front of Jessica; then Monica told Jess, "It's your turn." I kissed Jessica deep and long—my baby mother. I kissed the queen again, Monica, my wife, so passionately. Jessica lay down and took a nap, Monica and I played chess. She won. Savannah was tired. She took a nap too. Monica and I went in the shower and made love. She asked me, "Do you love your wife?" Monica and I went to bed. We all slept peacefully. The whole family did. We had a long day. Monica and Jessica grow closer together; the titles wife and baby mother were for people stuck in the matrix; we were a constellation. Both women understood the meaning of grand rising. The three of us realized our purpose was as energy beings inside of fleshly bodies. As my family slept, I lay awake thinking about every moment of my life. My great asset was the womb, even though I had spent most of my life honoring gold, cars, music, entertainment. We fight over countries, resources, and culture—it's the same as cartoons and toys. We're playing ourselves over things with no value. Grand rising has become a bumper sticker or slogan a campaign rally. I've heard stories and watched many movies about secret vampires; the funny thing is that monsters, aliens, vampires, and zombies are real, just like the devil. The silver screen creates a humorous narrative that these things are just an idea in the horror section of Block-buster. We were living that life, fighting the powers of the rul-ing class—a real invisible war is taking place. The ruling class is the vampires' feigners to our planet; the zombies are the general public who eat, sleep, and shit during a real alien invasion; the public is drinking beer and watching sports, going to church, and running a cash register. We returned to the states and went straight home to have a meeting about our grand rising. Monica, Jessica, and I talked about our real state of being. We couldn't fight over the domestic state-sponsored foolishness like "he's my man," child support, and cheating. Grand rising is the school that trains newly awakened energy beings to the knowledge of self; we're the only thing standing in the way of the aliens taking over the sleeping population. Knowledge of self is the transfer of information from our previous life in the universe. We came to Earth to stop the reptilians. The reptilians use the color white under the veil of white supremacy and religious differences, civil rights, and freedom; it's fool's gold. The entire planet is under the control of a blood-sucking death star. Monica made us some coffee. We stayed up talking about our vague recollection of life in the constellation. The three of us had implants in our mouth, so we didn't speak using words, just frequencies. Learning to use our chakras wasn't easy. All our strengths were different and based on how well we could align our chakras with the stars; our melanin powered our chakras. Monica had more experience than Jessica and me. Ms. Virginia had taught Monica many things. We spent most of our time together after work. It was vital before we could go in public. The system was trained to spot us. The cartoon *X-Men* was made. Our melanated people, the system used our color to disguise. It's why so-called people of color are targeted. We are the mutants in real life. Most of us die before we realize who we are and our capabilities; the key to controlling our power is to align the chakras. The system is an artificial organism that is growing on us and blocks the frequencies coming from the constellation through the sun and reprogramming us with signals of Saturn through the moon. As we arrive through the womb, the transmission between the sun and us is broken. There are many ways to take in transmission frequencies, such as walking barefoot and eating plants. Both of these things have been blocked. Genetically modified organisms are used to reprogram us; candy, ice cream, and sweets are generally used as biological weapons. From the outside looking in, people see two women and sexual pleasure. Our genders are just roles in a bigger reality. We're melanated beings using our genders as vehicles in Pangaea. I went back to work and focused on the job. We had a new family that took over the Copacabana. Jessica and Monica spent lots of time together. we communicated regularly through telepathy. The women were mentally stronger than me. Jessica and Monica came to love each other and proved to be most useful to each other as sisters. I was happy to see them growing together. Jessica was about nine months' pregnant and needed Monica and myself for support. The new family that took over the Copacabana changed our operation and fired Pauly and Vinnie. They been with us for years. Pauly was late every day, but we knew he worked hard and was reliable. Vinnie was slow, but he knew all of our customers in the community. Mikey and I were left. Bobby had six months before he retired. The company threw Bobby a party bash that rivaled the 1970s disco era. We danced the night away. We played MFSB's "TSOP (the Sound of Philadelphia)" (1973). He deserved it— thirty-five years on the job. Everybody dressed in 1970s disco clothes. Jessica and Monica had afros. Jessica was getting down at nine months' pregnant. The best part of the party was that we formed a soul train line, and Bobby danced down the line. What a night to remember. Shalamar's "A Night to Remember" was the last song to play. After Bobby retired, he moved back to Italy. I cried for days; he was like the father I never had. The Copacabana wasn't the same. People started leaving one after the other. My days were numbered. Things just weren't the same. The new family that took over the company had new ideas, most of which weren't legal. I went from delivering food to God knows what. The new guys on the block paid more. A different crowd started coming there. Since I worked at the Copacabana, no fights had ever happened; once the new family took over, shoot-outs and fights were practically every week. The community had respected Bobby. We never needed armed security. Now with the new family, everybody was packing, even Mikey. I learned a valuable lesson: nothing should last forever; you'll never appreciate it. Bobby was a legend; that man had soul.

People always said, "Remember the good old days when Bobby was here?" From 1968 until the 1990s, Bobby changed the community. He gave everyone an opportunity if you were willing to work for it. Bobby the Great. I'm just glad I had the chance to run with him. What a classic guy. The Copacabana wasn't diverse anymore. When Bobby was in charge, any given night you could find any flavor. I promised Bobby I and the family would visit him, and we will. That Sunday Jessica had the baby at home. Monica and I delivered the baby girl, Samantha. That's what I called teamwork. I was so proud of Jessica. She did that. Two years later our family was growing. We went through problems like every family. The only difference is we had a plan, and it was working. Monica and I planned the perfect wedding. We saved up two years. We invited all the family we could trace. My mother and father came, and so did sisters. We had over five hundred guests. Jessica helped us. We had the reception at the Copacabana. That was the best night of our lives. We had an all-black wedding with a touch of gold. Even our cake was black. Monica was and always will be my best friend. I loved Monica with my heart and soul. Bobby came back to walk Monica down the aisle. Both of us walked to the Johnson Brother's "Strawberry Letter 23." I cried on my wedding night. Monica had made me an honest man. Our lives were just getting started. That year Monica got her judgeship. She looked so beautiful in her black robe. I was so proud of my wife. She was my hero. The following year, Monica, Jessica, and I opened a restaurant. Our family model was if you controlled your income, you controlled your outcome. The kids were growing. My Aunt Karen and Jessica sister worked part time to help us. Savannah was four years old, and Samantha was going on two. Jessica got pregnant again. Our last baby was a boy. We named him Hezekiah. Monica and Jessica had a strong sisterhood. They supported each other. Jessica completed nursing school and became a registered nurse. I was impressed with their relationship, and the kids benefited the most—or maybe I did. All I know is that we were always happy. We made time for our family. Everybody needed one another. We had the conference and the powerful family. Our chemistry got so good. Hell, we had some great nights, especially when it rained. We put the kids to bed. Monica, Jessica, and I loved board games. When in the house, they trained me very well and made it clear there would be no outside influence. We meditated together researched and studied together. We were the black *Three's Company*. I grew stronger only because of Monica and Jessica, my left and right hand. I loved the way they ran the house. They were so connected. As we grew, so did our enemies. We figured out how to destroy the moon. No weapon on this planet could do it. Once we disconnected from the control of the moon, we worked together to unplug others. I became a scientist. I studied every particle I could under the sun and in the abyss. Monica knew every law and article of the system. Jessica knew the anatomy and biology. Our job to destroy the moon wasn't easy. We traveled the world freeing the minds of melanated people. Every person we removed from the control of the moon shrunk in size. The control the moon had over us kept the moon in the sky. The bigger the grand rising, the smaller the moon. Everywhere we went, the reptilians were there to keep the veil of ignorance over the people's eyes, to keep Saturn transmitting to the moon in the sky. We waited until our children were old enough and we were strong enough. We ran into Sabrina again in her lizard form. We destroyed her in the daylight. We set the trap using Tina. Monica, Jessica, and I stirred in the sun for one hour. With the rays of the sun, we transferred melanin into her body by looking at her. She overheated. Her skin begin to burn from the sun. We sent her back to her mothership moon. Then more people on Pangaea woke up and began to take in knowledge of self and grand rise; the moon lost control; the frequencies of Saturn weren't computing to the human mind anymore. The moon was sucking the energy from us like a battery, giving it the power to stay in our orbit. The more people that disconnected, the smaller the moon got. The reptilians created the program called civilization; the idea was to have people over time become dumbed down. turning them into routers, misleading and miseducating one another like a virus. Once the moon loses its power, the chain is broken. The future is a trap. Nothing gets better. The key is to go backward and reverse the damage civilization and technology have done. They are turning humans into cyborgs and dehumanizing melanated beings. The three of us loved the power of the sun. Civilization is a container that keeps people believing the future has something to offer, when the past is the remedy. The future only gets worse. Civilization is the umbrella; under it is religion, education, politics, and history. The systems of Saturn are designed to look like nature or enlightenment. Education doesn't mean illumination; it's a certificate or degree of information. Most times education is miseducation. History is another one of the constructed ideas created by Saturn to look like Pangaea, or natural. History is simply his story: dead trees; life turned into misinformation, taught by experts in deception. Monica, Jessica, and I weren't stuck in our lower selves. One might think two beautiful women sounds like a great threesome. No. What made us great is that we loved one another and saw the bigger picture. We had a whole planet being invaded by reptilians. The reptilians used the people of light skin, so-called white people, to create a substory: fools fighting over civil right, better education, and housing, Meanwhile the planet Pangaea is being taken over by reptilians. Monica and Jessica loved each other more than petty ninety-nine-cent issues. Their sisterhood was strong. That was a turn-on. My wife and baby mother were superheroes. The trick of Saturn is to create a laundry list of foolishness that person fought over annually. The moon is also a timer. It creates the idea of being busy, rushing. Once it's gone, there is no time, and that's the key. It's killing us; time is aging us. The moon is a death star. Once it's destroyed, time goes with it. Time is a mind-set. As an example, a person doing life in jail could care less about time. At that point they are free; the only problem is they don't have the sunlight. Monica and Jessica understood we were from the sun visiting on the earth, or Pangaea, but that didn't stop us from visiting the church. My mother invited my family Sunday morning to come and worship together. I was raised up in Brooklyn

Tabernacle under the great apostle Johnny Washington. The church had always been in the past a vehicle for the mothership. Apostle Johnny Washington was on his eighth solar return. Apostle Johnny Washington was from Canis Major, a constellation in the southern celestial hemisphere. Some call it heaven or the Dog Star. Many people are beginning to understand the Bible is a message in a message. The term *dog whistle* comes from the Dog Star. Its secrets are hidden in plain sight—the ability to speak in front of someone, but they are not able to comprehend totally. What people don't know is the entire world is in layers that you see, what you hear, and the reality. Monica, Jessica, the three children, and I had a wonderful time at church with my mother. She was showing everybody her grandbabies and daughters-in-law. My mother was proud of me. I had a successful family that got along. The kids were happy. Most of all, everyone had peace. We participated like everybody else, singing and shouting. We always brought our food with us wherever we went. At first friends and family found it to be weird, but we just told everyone we had a special diet. That worked. After church, everybody went over to my mother's house so the grandbabies could spend some time with my mother. Our bond was so abnormal to fools, the way you see others handling themselves. Jessica and Monica were working together and helping each other—just magical. Most of the beings on the planet Pangaea didn't notice the moon was missing. Instantly crime dropped. Wars were a thing of the past. People didn't age. The stayed. The average life span was 150 years. Slowly funeral company went out of business, and so did pharmaceutical companies. The moon was responsible for it all.

APOSTLE JOHNNY, WASHINGTON MOON LIFE

Time wasn't needed anymore. Neither were the days of the week and the calendar. They had become useless. The beings on Pangaea stopped eating meat, capitalism, democracy, communism, culture, religion—all of it was removed—never to control free beings again. The trick of Saturn was revealed. The only way this planet could break free from the control of Saturn was to destroy the moon; once the signal was broken, the moon couldn't deliver death anymore. The sun would make sure you lived, and the moon would make sure you died. Saturn controlled every aspect of life; every sense of mankind had been created by the reptilians. Law, marriage, religion, politics, culture, history, education, entertainment, the banking system, currency, media—think of them as colors in a crayon box. The name of the box is civilization. This box of Saturn is called civilization. History is blue; religion is yellow; politics is red. The idea is to paint a false narrative of nature, using the moon to cast a spell of radioactive frequencies, like a Wi-Fi signal controlling every being as a device. Angels and demons are just them versus us, good versus evil, and God versus the devil. The grand rising is beautiful. Life on Pangaea was meant to be a paradise; no being should pay for anything on Middle-Earth. Knowledge of self is the most important gift you can give to anyone; when intelligent beings know the self, none of the colorful programs works on them. The war between good and evil is real. On another level, what makes the war so crazy is that 90 percent of the world doesn't know it's happening. I think most people shouldn't know what's going on. The reality of what's going on will frighten the bravest. It takes a real effort not to let this system destroy us; persons fear groups like the Masons and other charter organizations because we believe they came up with the knowledge we see them displaying. Slavery is a great example of history and black people giving whites more credit than they deserve; slavery is and was a well-organized operation put together by beings higher than mankind, the reptilians. When people reflect on slavery, they assume white people are intelligent enough to create a system so complex. Saturn is the power behind what we call white supremacy, so truthfully we shouldn't fear mankind; he's just taking orders from reptilians in the corporate office of Saturn. It's amazing to see generations after generations misdiagnose the problem on our planet. Some say it's the devil; others say it's racism, or it's civil rights or religion or politics. I say it's all of the above. Saturn control them all. Out of one comes many. Now we know what that means. It's amazing how much misinformation is circulating in our minds. We're completely lost, without a clue. The idea that people believe there's something in the future to look forward to is ludicrous on its face. The saddest thing I ever have seen is people looking toward the future for a better life while at the same time looking inti the past for a time when peace was abundant in the land. This is the very meaning of magic. When one first starts the journey into grand rising, the stress level is overwhelming because one looks for support among the blind, looking to faith-based leaders and health officials just to find out they're apart of the Saturn system. I learned so many things from my wife; the most important is to balance the key ingredient in life. So many things make no sense until the bigger picture is shown to us. For now, the idea that secret societies are causing all of this damage to the planet helps us sleep at night—as long as we can blame somebody (the devil, the white man, the big pharmaceutical companies, racist police). It was too much to believe it was an alien presence until I studied law and what we call history. That's when it became clear no human or mankind could come up with this kind of wickedness on display in Middle-Earth today. After we left my mother's house, Monica, Jessica, and I went home to perform a ritual. We were learning how to shape-shift. Jessica came up with the idea of dancing our way into different portals in time. Pangaea had placed many star gates or portals on Middle-Earth. Some of the star gates could take one beyond the underworld to the abyss or above the heavens past the firmament; the star gates were only accessible to shape-shifters by mental frequencies. We marvel over the technology mankind has brought forward; our ancestors were far more advanced. Just imagine beings traveling in time and to different corners of Middle-Earth just by walking through a waterfall or entering into a certain mountain during a quarter moon. Monica came up with the idea of time traveling while making love; these things take practice, and we worked on them for years. We got better at them and stronger. We were not a perfect family. The hardest part of our life was remembering to blend in with society. The only bond stronger than a man and a woman is a family, so the message to you, the reader, is don't let this system suck you into it like *Ghostbusters*. Yes we have to fight the powers that be, but our happiness and mental wellness is important. With the moon gone, things changed quickly. People on Middle-Earth began answering their own questions. The system around the people slowly disappeared, like the police department, insurance companies, and the fire department. Even cell phones became obsolete. Most of these devices were control checkpoints. The system created things in our life to look essential, like police, grocery stores, and clinics. Most of us were born in a zoo-like environment, and nothing makes sense. But how would one know if everybody around you doesn't complain? We begin to believe the things we see are normal. So the ghetto is a normal jail full of black, called a minority, is normal; living in a rich neighborhood two blocks down from a poor neighborhood is perfectly normal. Growing up in my so-called community was the only standard I could judge the world by. As I grew up and traveled to other states, where the so-called black community was located, I quickly learned the difference between a black community and a heavily black populated area. A dysfunctional group of people can't live in a community. The conditions that created damaged people through slavery, jim crow, sharecropping, colonization. Without systematic rhyme or any reparative, isolated justice creates a never-ending cycle of crime and predators, a mentally ill herd of animals resembling people. When you don't know what the human being is and how it's made, then you can't know when it's broken. We're electric beings or computers in flesh. None of us would take our cell phone or car to church, so why do we take ourselves? We don't know we're electric beings, and a device like a moon was made to be a wireless router for the signal frequencies coming from Saturn, which are controlling us. Of course this seems far out when you've spent your whole life watching *Sesame Street*, singing your ABCs, hoping to go to Disney Land, and watching Saturday morning cartoons. This isn't *The Twilight Zone*; this is very real. Now, to me, the devil burning people in hell seems way crazier than the moon, which you can see, controlling life on the planet. The Bible stories are self-explanatory, a collection of artificial stories with actors and actress following a script, and you get to play along. The Bible is a litmus test for the scientist and governments of the world. If you can believe in the stories in that book, you'll believe anything except the truth. So we're walking into the concept called the future, which is a graveyard. As long as we believe the future is bringing us better days, we'll remain the frog in the pot cooking on a low flame; the future is another one of the control devices made by Saturn. This Rubik's Cube of an idea has taken us far too long to figure out; the puzzle, the past, is the only hope for Pangaea. The beings on Middle-Earth that are below the firmament and above the abyss have no idea what's going on and nowadays prefer not to. It's too much work. Nobody has time for fresh food—give us a microwave. Time makes us compromise. Why farm when there are pharmaceuticals, TV dinners, frozen food, and whatnot? The old saying proves wise today: they who would let themselves be fooled, let them. The truth is not welcomed in this world under the control of Saturn; the lie is the standard we live by. For many, it's too late to reverse the damage. We're talking about generations of misinformation inculcated into our membrane. I had many years to discern life: what's real and fake and the propaganda and wishful thing that permeate everyday living. Tomorrow is always worse than today. Keeping it real and bullshitting run on the same track; the light at the end of the tunnel is a train. The simple things in life are what was before civilization and history. Pleasure at the expense of others—pain—is the way this world is built. Capitalism, democracy, and religion are no different than sports—this team versus that team. One valuable lesson I learned painfully was not to keep sharing information with persons that have the same access to knowledge as I do. Truth is like a menu. People can choose what they want on their plate; after all, it's free will. Life is messed up when 90 percent of the world when asked how are they doing, say, "I'm surviving." I was the person trying to save people by offering what I knew about God; then I realized the only way to know about God is to study her creation. God can't be contained in a book or library. The people who tell you about God need the most help and know the least. They never travel and don't realize God is science; the world is a small, simple place, but left up to our imagination (movie directors), God is whatever you can understand: the old one-two punch I call shampoo and conditioner, religion and politics. We're Christian and Democrats at birth. That never bothered me at first until I began to track the process of how the entire black so-called community finds itself in mental conditions like the one we're under. It starts with our childhood, harmlessly baptized and christened. What we don't see is that we're being offered up as a sacrifice and registered under a secret society. Our parents take an oath to live by the agreement, so we're born again, baptized, under a new mother and father; church is our mother, and the state is our father. This process gives our local government authority over our beings. The only way to reverse this covenant is to join a secret society and make a new contract. In buying back our freedom, from birth, we become a part of the new slave trade. In return, our guardians or parents gain access to the system's education and workforce. This is the new mark of the beast. This is a brilliant plan most of us will never realize because we're under the veil of ignorance, thinking the church is an organization that leads people to good, not the devil. Monica and Jessica studied the biblical scripture regularly every week. I was amazed at what the book actual says; it explains the contract with the devil and notifies us about the truth of our faith. The bible is very clear that Jesus and Satan are the same.

People read the truth of Jesus and the devil as the same character and say to themselves, "There must be another explanation for what we just read because what we learned about Jesus from our local church, they didn't say anything about this, and my parents told me Jesus was good and the devil was evil." The same thing happens to us with our country. We're told America is fighting for freedom even though we went through four hundred years of slavery. Once we figure out the real reason America is fighting all these wars and that we're the evil ones, in disbelief many take their lives. We realize we're a part of the problem and have been lied to our entire lives. Most of the time we wake up after the damage is done, and we've helped to kill so many innocent people that now we can't leave the dark side. Religion works the same way. By the time you read the entire Bible a few times, all of your questions come with answers. We can't handle the truth. It's easier to ignore the truth and tell yourself that this can't be. So we travel back in our history, starting with our slavery, then Africa colonization, then the rest of the world, and the truth could be more obvious; then we run back to the Bible, looking for God to make sense of this whole thing.

Then you ask yourself, "Where did I get this Bible from, and who wrote it? And who's King James?" Now by this time you need medication and are depressed, but you can't tell anybody because they haven't discovered what you have. They're under the veil of ignorance and will think you're losing it or the devil is in you. Most of our families will report us to the local authorities thinking they're helping us; then the only safe haven becomes the street, as we call it. The gangs and drugs are waiting for our welcome to the never-ending story. The truth doesn't set anyone free; it drives you crazy and leaves more questions than answers. That's where we learn the truth about Saturn, the author of all systems. This world is very confusing until one receives a grand rising to understand the real creator. When the constellation reveals the truth, it's also right in front of our eyes; just like the sun and the moon, there is no excuse for us to blame the universe, God, for being under the veil of ignorance because the real truth is so obvious. This is the test. All things in plain sight make your decision. The universe owns and controls the skies. The evidence must be clear and visible for all to see. There is one main law and two underlaws. The universe, God, controls the law of the heavens; mankind controls the law of the land and water.

THE CREATOR IN PLAIN SIGHT

The rule of the universe overrules the law of Saturn. Mankind has the right to confuse and mislead Middle-Earth using books, universities, movies, and music. The heavens displayed the facts about the Creator under the dome; the facts about the creator are also in the abyss. The law of heaven states no being can be responsible for the ignorance of the law until the beings reach the age of thirteen. The being must be given time to observe the stars. The reptilians start the process of miseducating the beings from the womb. The education, entertainment, and religious systems imprison the mind and redirect the being's destiny. What we're born to do and know are overshadowed by career, family, politics, and civil service. Cartoons and toys have one purpose: to relegate the mind to a lower frequency. Let us be clear: from the time you come out of the womb, the system of Saturn has the authority to test you using food, education, fun—any bait possible that can confine a human being to the prison cell inside its self, called Tartarus. The constellation reveals the real purpose of the universal God through our melanin; the sun speaks to us in frequencies, drawing our attention to the message of the stars, so the reptilians started spraying the skies to break the communication. The war between good and evil is just a metaphor for the sun versus the moon. The two spaceships are at war for control over Middle-Earth, a secret hidden in plain sight. The church and state worked together for years to make sure human beings never noticed the signs in front of their faces in the heavens. The church made it a sin to observe the astrology of the stars. The reasoning made no sense, but like everything else, we just excepted it until we could no longer avoid the obvious truth. That is why time is given to every being. The sun is influencing life; the moon is influencing death. Over time the ancient world created the religious story of light versus dark, evil with a *D*, good without the extra *O*, the Son of God, the light of the world, the four seasons that became the four gospels, the twelve months that became the twelve disciples. The Bible is full of truth and falsehoods. Astrotheology has been the basis of all religions, in-your-face reality turned into stories based on allegories. The further one researches into religions, one finds that all the characters in the Bible were at one point astrological symbols. The relationship between theocracy and astrotheology is almost identical; it's very difficult for people to accept the truth of the constellation, being the way we have become the People of the Book, and somehow we can accept the perversion of every aspect of life partially. The person under slavery notices everything given to them during that slavery period, from education to food and justice, was no good. The only good thing they ever received as slaves was religion. That's the sad truth of people's denial. We've been hexed; this vicious cycle continues from generation to generation. The veil of ignorance, the blindfold, is placed over our eyes by our parents, so there's no reason to fight until now. The greatest story ever told through a book written by mankind has become the word of God. Most people have never studied etymologies, so everything they read is taken at face value, as is the justice system. It is the same way people with money or education are the most ignorant and the first to awaken to the truth. Saturn is behind every institution, from sports to marriage, entertainment, politics, news, radio, and religion. Think of these items as apps or websites, and civilization as your web browser. No person can participate in any avenue of life unless the being is orientated into civilization. This is why we watch television, and our favorite basketball players or wrestler and singers have people behind them we don't see until we're older; then we learn who owns the NBA, record labels, and TV networks. The world we're presently living in is opposed to the truth out of embarrassment and/or fear; the truth is the only thing on this planet that can take away our fear of the reptilians and mankind under the control of Saturn. The lie is designed in such a way that people are afraid to know the truth because governments or religious leaders, even family, will reject you; in some cases, people HAVE even lost their lives for speaking truth to power. So it's easier to just put everything in the hands of God, whoever that might be, not knowing we're being tested, and every being must accept the truth and reject the lie. This means most of the time going against a relative's friend's family traditions. One could ask the question, How did Saturn gain this kind of control over us? My answer is the same: others control our emotions. We allow it, just like the moon is powerless once Middle-Earth wakes up and doesn't allow the moon to harness our energy, the same way viruses and bacteria use our body against us. Saturn grows stronger the more people are ignorant and dumbed down to the level of just a battery, Saturn feeds off of fear, ignorance, hate, death, and wickedness. The moon is just a microphone that broadcasts the message on a frequency translator. Just like Wi-Fi signals translate to our device without our knowing there's Wi-Fi around us, the moon translates a similar frequency. This artificial hollowed planetoid, known as the moon disk, operates the same way. Therefore, people who have spent their whole lives watching Bugs Bunny, drinking beer, and paying bills can't even comprehend the elementary control Saturn has over us. This all sounds like sci-fi even though its right in our faces. The book should seem like sci-fi, but that is the power of Saturn, to turn what is real into a GMO. Saturn has turned our entire Middle-Earth into GMOs. Food, plants, and religious belief systems are all artificial, and the people wouldn't know the difference if you told them. So, you see, we have the power to stop Saturn if the people of Middle-Earth break the frequency of the moon connecting us to Saturn. This is easier said than done. People can't handle the truth. It's too bright. This leads me to my next point. What do the stars have to do with the truth? Everything. They're not just navigation and decor for a nice outdoor dinner party. The stars are constellations of messages placed in the heavens for all to see. Nobody should be able to say they have been deceived, but when people have been dumbed down to not even notice the food they're eating is fake or how their anatomy works, it would make perfect sense that they can't see what's in the sky. The system we live in is upside down and inside out. From the small spectacle of truth, it makes no sense to those blinded by Saturn. For example, every man has a belly button and was created from a woman, but the system, religious or not, supports such a foolish idea. Just think of the mind control you must have over a people that you could convenience them. A woman came from a man's rib. That's an insult to the grand architectural science of common sense, and nature makes this point very clear. These are the very points of fact that keep Middle-Earth stagnant; this is one of the biggest miseducations of Saturn to support a completely crazy litmus test. Again, if you can believe women come from men, you can believe anything. Black women are the beginning of life when the world can't come to terms with the facts of life; their problem is with God. The only thing every man can agree on in Middle-Earth is that man was created first. Something is wrong with that picture. Every child born on Pangaea must be made to learn that truth: man was created first. God must be addressed by "he" or "him"; this fundamental truth is more important than we know. In the

holy books of the Abrahamic men of the covenant, they concluded there are three main pillars to keeping the veil of ignorance over the eyes of the elected. The Abrahamic men of the
covenant work together to make sure the entire earth believes
that (1) God is in the image of a man, (2) the earth is round, and
(3) God is found in a book. Which book? Eeny, meeny, miny,
moe. We spend our whole lives trying to figure that one out.
These three pillars are the bedrock or mission statement of Saturn. Now just think what the world would look like if we re-
versed our thinking. So God would be a woman, and the earth
would be flat, and God would not be in a book. We just solved
half the problems of the world and exposed the wicked teachings
of Saturn. Look how easy that was. And there's tons of evidence
to prove we've been lied to. When the mind is bent to see things
that are not there or believe things that make no sense at all, like
telling black Americans that July 4, 1776, is our Independence
Day or we're African American with no dual citizenship. What
about "all men are created equal" at the same time the founders
of the United States of America had slaves? My personal favorite
in the Garden of Eden is that Eve talked to a snake. These are
just a few of the IQ tests that are given to the general public to
make sure we're still sleeping. Again, if you can believe those
things, we'll fall for anything, like voting for the left wing or the
right wing. Why is Saturn doing this, and why doesn't Saturn
just take over Middle-Earth already? What's the holdup? Remember, even in the Bible, the devil was given instructions and
limitations. Saturn can't destroy Middle-Earth, but it wants human beings to destroy it. Saturn can only control us through the
moon and using devices of our free will; therefore, we're enslav-

ing ourselves with our signature on everything we do. Saturn follows the rule of the universe, which states that we must be fully aware of what we're doing and given notice, just like in the judicial system. The idea is to trick us into a fake contract or give us notice in the fine print. Another trick of Saturn is a language with double meanings. The United States of America's nickname should be "double meaning." The reason why Saturn is testing us is that we're the most intelligent beings ever produced, so we should be able to figure out a few cheap tricks. Saturn's claim to our test is if the truth was so clear and black and white, we would never believe the earth was round versus flat or that man created woman. Surely God as found in the book would be foolishness to us intelligent beings. Saturn's claims are very strong. The grand created is a liar; we don't have free will; we believe whatever we're told. Sadly the entire planet has been dumbed down to a level lower than animals. We didn't come from monkeys, but we're turning into monkeys. This is where our leaders come into play. Saturn is the mastermind behind the whole operation. The firmament prevents Saturn from entering into our orbit, so the moon has to act as a loudspeaker and transmitter. The reptilians are the direct servants of Saturn and the only ones allowed to go to the moon to receive firsthand technology to enslave Middle-Earth; in return, our leaders receive information and superior knowledge from what we have on our planet. This is seen in Greek mythology and ancient Rome—gifts from the gods. Saturn rewards its servants well, with knowledge of how to create guns, television, missiles, tanks, cell phones, light bulbs, and computers. All of these devices are destroying Middle-Earth, and we're walking ourselves into prison; the latest technology is one step closer to our permanent enslavement, and we don't even realize it. The intelligence we have on Middle-Earth comes from the moon or the sun. Every time mankind comes from the moon, Middle-Earth jumps to another level; each step is the dawn of a new day, or what we call the New World Order, a world vastly different from the natural founding of Middle-Earth, a dehumanized cyborg world everything is genetically modified. We are the undoing of ourselves with the assistance of Saturn and the reptilians. The only way to stop Saturn is to destroy the frequency of the moon coming from Saturn. Monica, Jessica, and I led the rebellion and disabled the moon, but this was only temporary. As we speak, they are working to recharge the moon using silver as a backup energy source. The moon is powered by the energy that comes from human beings; our energy is drained by our ignorance and miseducation and redistributed to the belief in Saturn. The sun is the opposite; it also is a transmitter for the universe and enlightens human beings. The sun is also a disk, and the reptilians and Saturn are trying to block the frequencies coming from the sun by spraying the skies and creating fake clouds.

SATURN TRICK, MOON DISK, SUN DISK

Black people invented many things on Middle-Earth with the help of the sun; it's the giver of every good gift. The sun used to be referred to as a black woman like everything else: Mother Nature; Mama Africa. Life is a bitch or woman. Most of the world today doesn't remember or can't handle the truth. The purpose of miseducating Middle-Earth is to reeducate the population; that's the only way to get humans to believe a woman came from a man or Middle-Earth is a round ball and not a flat disk. The objective of Saturn is to destroy the mind and rebuild it; this has worked like a charm. That's why I was sent here from the mothership, to remove the veil of ignorance from the eyes of the dumb, deaf, and blind. Saturn doesn't know when we're coming, but they know the only way into Middle-Earth is through the womb. So Saturn has been attacking the black women, getting the reptilians to make mankind pass laws on abortion and, at the same time, creating the conditions for the women to want an abortion of their free will. The knowledge of Saturn reviled to all in Middle-Earth removes the veil from their eyes. The moon will fall into the ocean, never to return, but that won't stop Saturn from building another one. Saturn has many moons built already. Without the reptilians and mankind to dumb down Middle-Earth, the other moons don't have the power to stay in our orbit. There was a time when three moons surrounded Pangaea; in my first solar visit, two of them were destroyed, and rings were placed around Saturn to confine the beings on the planet disk from leaving. So they created moons, objects that look natural enough to be in plain view without our knowing. In the ancient world, people knew what they were. They called them death stars. The name came from the size of the moons—they used to blend in with the stars. When that didn't work anymore, Saturn created a moon the size of the sun that confused most of the people on Middle-Earth. There are many books and documentaries from many nations and tribes that talk about the time before the moon. Saturn is where the idea of Satan comes from—another idea to blind the minds of the people on Middle-Earth. This idea of Satan is one of the greatest deceptions of Saturn, to keep the minds of intelligent beings fixated on the greatest story ever told. What is another word for *story*? *Lie*. Saturn is called the father planet of the lie, as we're called Mother Earth or Pangaea, meaning "the truth." Saturn knows its time has come to an end. The reptilians and mankind were given three ages to prove their claims, each age being 2,020 years, three zodiacs. The first of the three ages was the Ice Age, then the Dark Age, and the last is the Golden Age. The reptilians call the last age the dawn of a new day, with the sun not able rise above the mountains. The three ages will last 6,060 years, then Middle-Earth will reset again. This time the reptilians and mankind will be removed from Pangaea, and the rings around Saturn, the lord of the rings, will remain for three eons. The truth will be restored. Time will be no more death and pain or funerals and hospitals. They will all be a thing of the past. History, civilization, and the future will no longer exist. Every day will be the present, and the only thing we'll look forward to is the past. Saturn will never deceive us again. Middle-Earth will heal no more culture and nationalities. Ethnicities, religion, education, governments, grocery stores, money, and corporations all will be removed. Our job is to open the mind's eye to the truth of what these things are and where they came from: Saturn. Everything we know, from marriage to school, church, and politics, all came from Saturn. No man or woman needs a license to be together as a family or a university to miseducate them or a religion to lead them to God or a politician to organize the collective. All of those systems are the works of Saturn.